Prais

MW01505583

"40" is a panorama of parables! A treasure trove of tales! All worth your time!"

— Scott Cottrell, author of *When Chaos Reigns*

"John Cleveland's 40 parables speak the truth with a creative modern-day twist that you will connect with and contemplate throughout the day."

— Shannon O'Shea, Deputy Director of Clearfield Job Corps Center

John Cleveland's compassion for people is evident in these creative, modern-day parables conveying biblical truths about the God who loves us.

— Tara Reimer, Registered Nurse, McKay-Dee Hospital

JC nails it with creative modern-day parables that brings us to the realization of what our JC's (Jesus Christ) nails did for us.

— John Gibson – Director of Serving You Ministries, Birmingham, AL

"In keeping with Jesus's tradition of sharing the Gospel with parables, John Cleveland serves us these forty vignettes, which offer fresh and entertaining perspectives of biblical truths. Exceptionally well crafted and spiced with whimsy, they are perfectly suited for consumption as daily devotionals. But although they are pleasing to the palate and readily digested, each sumptuous offering packs a substantial helping of spiritual insight and encouragement. Bon appetit!"

— MIKE JENNE, AUTHOR OF *BLUE GEMINI*, *BLUE DARKER THAN BLACK* AND *PALE BLUE*

40 is a fantastic collection of short stories that skillfully weave together humor, relatability, and faith. Each tale is masterfully crafted, showcasing the author's talent in capturing the complexities of human imperfection and the divine grace that permeates our lives. The more I read these stories, I found myself drawn into moments of contemplation, laughter, and deep reflection on the love and mercy of our Savior. The author's ability to blend humor with profound spiritual insights is truly remarkable, reminding readers of the beautiful truth that God truly has a sense of humor and works through our flaws to accomplish His purposes. I couldn't put this book down; it's a must-read for anyone seeking inspiration and a touch of joy in their journey of faith.

— KYLE HILL – EXECUTIVE PASTOR OF THE GENESIS PROJECT, OGDEN, UTAH

40

A Collection of Modern-Day Parables

John Cleveland

Publish Authority

40: A Collection of Modern-Day Parables
ISBN 978-1-954000-77-3 (Paperback)
ISBN 978-1-954000-78-0 (eBook)

Editor: Janet Silburn
Cover design lead: Raeghan Rebstock

Published 2024, by Publish Authority
300 Colonial Center Parkway, Suite 100
Roswell, GA 30076-4892 USA
PublishAuthority.com

Printed in the United States of America

CONTENTS

Dedicated with eternal gratitude to Randy who patiently yet persistently introduced a nineteen-year-old soldier to the Truth. It has made all the difference.

People forget facts, but they remember stories.

— Joseph Campbell

FOREWORD

John Cleveland has produced a book not only worthy of your purchase and reading, but each of his stories, his allegories, his parables, if you will, have a life and message of their own.

Each story is short, frequently humorous, and thought provoking. John's dry wit comes through these life lessons loud and clear, enhancing their central messages of faith, hope, and love.

I have known John for several years and am always impressed by his honesty, thoughtfulness, directness, and faith in God. I consider him a friend whose opinion I seek.

From "Absent Manager " to "Worms Aplenty," you will enjoy each parable while reflecting on your own life and their own obvious (and some not-so-obvious) parallels. Each tale will challenge you to consider those parallels in a new light—not that of a condemning police interrogation room with a single light bulb hanging overhead but a bright yet soft and warm light inviting you to consider your life, faith, faults, and attributes.

I assure you that you will find yourself described accurately in at least one of these 40 stories, if not many more. So slow down, step out of the rat race for a few hours, and get lost in these 40 short adventures.

You will not regret it and might even learn some things about yourself.

Scott B. Cottrell
Colonel, US Army (Ret)
Author of *When Chaos Reigns: A Political Thriller*

INTRODUCTION

So, what exactly is a modern-day parable? Just like a speaker delivering an illustration, they are tools to help us grasp concepts. I don't think that mine are divinely inspired. God has yet to speak to me audibly, so these are simply the fruits of my imagination. However, Steve Harvey says, "Your gift is the thing you do at your absolute best with the least amount of effort." I like to talk about faith. I like to tell stories. I wanted to share them with you.

These stories began several years ago while I was volunteering as a chaplain at Serving You Ministries in Birmingham, Alabama. Not all of our clients had a working knowledge of the Bible, and it was safe to say that none of them were professional farmers, fishermen, or shepherds. With that in mind, I began to make up stories like the parables in the Bible but used modern-day themes instead. They incorporated cruise ships, pet dogs, celebrities, coffee, and even space travel. After a while, my wife said that I should write them down. Having benefited from her wisdom and intuition over the years, I said, "Yes ma'am!" and began to type.

The collection of stories continues to grow but I've selected

40 to share with you. Why 40? It is a number that has repetitive significance in the Bible. Plus, I thought it would be cool to have a title that consists only of numbers. Please read these with a light heart and open mind. They are seldom serious and make no claim to have theological depth (or even accuracy!). My hope is that they will stir your imagination and cause you to ponder the unseen forces that many of us suspect are at work within us and in the world around us. And my prayer is that they will benefit you and honor our Heavenly Father.

Happy reading!

1. Absent Manager

Joe pulled the lever for cocoa powder and watched the brown dust fall into his little white cup. He looked around and grinned because he had secret information. You see, he had discovered that the hot beverage machine would dispense hot cocoa, or coffee, or cider (or whatever) whether or not you put coins in it.

Sometimes, Joe would sit in the break room pretending to read the paper but would secretly watch all the suckers put quarter after quarter into the defunct device. *Bunch of saps,* he would say to himself. *People are so gullible and naïve. They all go through the motions of life, doing what they're supposed to without questioning anything. They never look for opportunities to get ahead.* He shook his head with superiority and disdain.

"Well, better be getting back to work," he said aloud. If his co-workers had followed him back to his workstation, they would have witnessed little to no work being done at all. But he had appearances to maintain. You never knew when there might be a peer review.

Before leaving the break room, he went back to the beverage machine and mimed pulling coins from his pocket and putting them in the slot. He filled one Styrofoam cup with hot chocolate and another with hot coffee. He thought, *Why not? It's free!*

He walked down the hall with a cup in each hand, contents sloshing dangerously close to the rim. He turned right into his division and noticed the new guy in the room to his right. The most recent employee, or "Rookie" as Joe liked to call him, had his back turned. His arms could be seen moving as he performed a complicated technical task on the table in front of him. The young man was dressed neatly, with his shirt tucked in around his slim waist. His neck was cleanly shaven to the collar line, and his shoes looked practical.

Joe couldn't resist a little playful banter, so he stopped at the entrance to the younger man's workspace. "What's up, Rook? You tryin' to upgrade the boss's boat with all your extra effort?"

The young man's measured movements stopped, and he turned around with a puzzled expression. His face showed that he recognized his older, more rotund, and...seasoned work neighbor. He smiled politely. "Morning! Yeah, I've got a lot to do today. These need to be ready to go by Friday. What about you? How's it going?"

The young man's niceness was oddly off-putting. After all, this was work. This was a place to complain about the supervisors, the pay, everyone around you, and about how you're being treated. "Friday, huh? So what happens if you don't get them done by Friday?"

The young man looked down and seemed to consider this. "Well, I guess some customers will be missing them, and I'm sure someone higher up won't be happy about that."

"But what about you? What happens to you if they don't get done by Friday?" His tone was as empty as the concern in his eyes.

"I don't know. I guess they could...write me up, or make me work over next week, or let me go."

"Wrong! They don't do nothin'." Joe's voice was suddenly rancorous. "They can't afford to. Do you know how hard it is for them to find some sap who will do this crap for the peanuts they pay? They're not gonna fire you. They're as lazy as everyone else who works here." His fingers made air quotes to emphasize the word "works." It was an odd gesture with the cups in each hand. Brown liquid spilled onto the floor and his already stained tie.

The young man's face registered disappointment. He seemed to be weighing his words or deciding if he should respond at all. "I actually like working here. There were other options, but I chose this one. I think it suits me." He turned slightly, indicating that he needed to get back to work.

The salty vet couldn't let it go. "Where is the boss? Do you think he sees the difference between me and you?" His tone had become crass and biting. "I don't see any security cameras. I don't see any walk-throughs by the supervisors. They don't care, so I don't care."

The contemplative young man asked, "But what about the paychecks?"

"What about 'em?"

"Well... I'd be upset if they stopped, so...I feel like I need to deserve them. You know, show that I appreciate them."

"Now you wanna talk about pay? The boss is a cheap bum. I barely have enough to make ends meet each month."

"That's interesting because we make more than employees at comparable businesses here in town. Have you had any better offers? Besides, there's more to this job than pay. It's stable, we get benefits, the work environment is clean...mostly." The young man's gaze accidentally dropped to the floor and Joe's soiled tie.

Reflexively, Joe looked straight down at the speckled fabric that hung from his neck. "Sap. You keep on bustin' your butt for The Man. Pay for his new boat or whatever hobby he has that keeps him away from here. It's obvious he doesn't care about this place...or us."

The young man paused to formulate his thoughts and then spoke. "So, what would it be like if the boss was here every day? And what if he watched you work? I mean, really watched. Looking over your shoulder, scrutinizing every move and decision. It'd be miserable, even for me."

"Well, maybe I'd be a better employee if he'd been a better boss. He doesn't give his best, so why should I?"

The young man's mind reeled to form a rational response. "What about the break room?"

"What about it?" Joe asked flatly.

"Why do we even have a break room? It wasn't stipulated in the contract we signed. But there it is...for us. And what about the bathrooms? Aren't they always stocked with soap and toilet paper? What about the Employee Appreciation Luncheon? Free steak? And what about the Christmas bonus? They don't even expect a thank you. They just give it whether you deserve it or not."

Joe frowned. The usual snappy comeback was not coming to his lips. He settled on something simple and snide. "You're a boy scout."

"Maybe so. But I have every reason to do a good job for the boss and no reason not to. If or when he decides to drop by, I want him to find me working."

Joe huffed with disgust. There would be no convincing this guy. "Sap," he muttered as he turned to leave. Besides, his coffee was getting cold.

2. All or Nothing

Emily remained in a sitting position, although the sleek sarcophagus was obviously shaped for a person to lie down. Suddenly reluctant, Emily spoke to a monitor that was affixed to an articulated mechanical arm situated in front of her.

"So, how long is this supposed to take?"

The screen answered in a voice that sounded completely human. "Seventy-seven years, six months, fourteen days, three hours, sixteen minutes. The seconds remain variable."

Emily paused to consider if it was worth worrying that the computer had used "fourteen days" instead of "two weeks."

"So would you wake me up if there was a problem, like, if we were going to crash?"

"Would you want me to?"

She considered this as well.

"It depends; I think I would want to be woken up if there was something I could do about it."

"When you say, 'doing something about it,' does that include potentially delaying the inevitable?"

The computer program was so pragmatic. Although it

excelled at calculating statistical probabilities, its bedside manner was less than comforting.

"Give me a hypothetical scenario where you would wake me up," Emily replied.

The computer responded almost instantaneously. "If there were an astronomical anomaly that would not be replicated in your lifetime, I would consider waking you, depending on its magnitude."

"What, you mean something unusual that I might want to witness? That doesn't sound like an emergency."

"You didn't specify emergencies. You inquired about scenarios."

"So, you wouldn't wake me up if we were about to collide with an asteroid, but you would wake me up for some cool scenery?"

"The basis of life is not simply sustainment or protection but the facilitation of experiential embedding in the hippocampus within your temporal lobe."

"Making memories? That's what you're telling me?"

The computer elaborated. "I could chemically sustain the anatomy of your organism, but that in itself would not constitute a human life. The essential factor is your consciousness, your ability to reason, create, make moral judgments, and, yes, make memories. They are the constructive basis for improved decision making, which increases the likelihood of enhanced memory making."

"So, at the end of my existence, my memories will determine the value of my life?"

"They will be the substance of your life, but their cumulative value is highly subjective. Also, there is the probability of continued existence beyond your current physical status."

"Are you telling me you have statistical proof that I have a soul?"

"The complexity of your existence exponentially exceeds that of your nearest biological relative, the chimpanzee, or even my own operating system. The unique nature of human consciousness demands the consideration of spiritual metaphysics."

They were drifting into deep waters. Emily decided to change the subject.

"So, tell me again about your asteroid avoidance program."

"As explained earlier, my advanced forward radar detects potential threats to the ship and uses the telemetry data to make adjustments to our trajectory."

"So, what happens if we have to make so many adjustments that we run out of fuel?"

"The ship is equipped with an adequate amount of propellant to complete the mission."

"And how much is that?"

"Seventy-seven years, six months, fourteen days, three hours, sixteen minutes' worth. The seconds remain variable."

"So, we only have just enough? What happens if we run out of gas anyway?"

The computer paused for an unusually long time. Emily found this worrisome. The monitor remained stone-faced as it calculated and prepared a response.

Finally, it answered. "I would wake you up."

She wasn't sure if the computer was joking. Emily slowly lay down and looked at the intravenous line into her arm. The hibernation protocol would not commence unless she gave her permission.

The computer spoke. "Your submission is the only remaining impediment to our departure."

Once she consented, she would be sedated for the duration of the flight...pending a really cool supernova or black hole. She would have to trust her safety to the ship and believe that it would navigate through any debris or at least survive a collision. It required complete surrender. But the fading probability of remaining alive on this ailing planet versus starting over in the future on New Earth limited her options. She lay back in the pod, took a moment to appreciate that she was worth saving, and gave the command.

"I'm all yours."

3. Autonomous Autos

I t was the interview of a lifetime. How could a rookie
reporter with a small paper have secured an audience with
Ethan Brusk? But it was happening. The receptionist had
actually called Louise by name, and security had not burst into
the room to drag her outside. It felt surreal. The break of a
lifetime. Sure, she had interviewed last year's Autumn Pumpkin
Contest winner and even a city council candidate. But this was
the big leagues. She considered which news syndicate might
purchase this piece and if it might appear in some national
publication. Her mind was racing, her palms were sweaty, and
nervous emotions emanated from her innards.

Louise changed her inner monologue to a pep talk. *Be
courteous but direct. Show confidence. He's used to meeting with
powerful people. Be one.*

The receptionist called Louise's name and pressed a button
on her desk as she walked towards a set of stylish double doors.
The locking mechanism buzzed, and one of the doors clicked
and softly opened on its own. *Of course, Ethan Brusk's doors
would open automatically.*

She walked into an impressive office, more like a suite, with jaw-dropping views of the city below. It was simple and elegant, understatedly modern. She felt giddy at seeing this international celebrity in the flesh...and having an audience with him! She stuck her hand out and tried to deliver the greeting she had been rehearsing.

"Thank you for brushing me, Mr. Meeting. Er... I mean, thank you for meeting me, Mr. Ethan, uh, Mr. Brusk."

A warm smile and chuckle. "Please, call me Ethan. And thank you! I've read some of your work. It's good."

Louise's face reflected the puzzlement that filled her mind as she pondered which of her articles Ethan Brusk could have possibly read and why. "Really? Which one?"

"It was about the firemen who babysat the kids after their parents had been in that car crash. Really touching. We actually sent the department a donation after reading about that."

"Wow! I'm flattered. And thank you." Louise took out a digital recorder and notepad. Time was fleeting, and she needed to seize the moment.

"Would you mind if we got started? I know your time is very valuable, and I want to squeeze in as much as we possibly can."

Ethan shrugged his shoulders, stretched his lips into a smile, and said, "There's no hurry, really. I've cleared my afternoon for this. I'm really a big fan."

How was this possible? How had one of the world's most wealthy and influential men not only known her name but also opened his schedule and offered accolades to a nobody like herself? Should she be honored? Should she be wary?

"Umm, thank you very much...for that. It's funny that you brought up car crashes because that's one of the things I wanted to ask you about."

Ethan nodded and looked up. "Yes. Obviously, I should expect some questions about that. As they say, 'The buck stops here.' So, let 'em rip."

No avoidance. No deflecting. Interesting. "You are a pioneer, more accurately, *the* pioneer of autonomous automobiles. You engineered the technology that allows the vehicles to move about the city and run errands without human input. It's the stuff we dreamed about when we were kids watching George Jetson. But in spite of these unprecedented advancements, there have been accidents."

More nodding but without breaking eye contact. "And?"

"And I thought you might like to respond to the criticism and accusations. Every major news outlet has been questioning your creation and accusing you of being out of control. It seems that some consider you a visionary captain of industry while the rest want you crucified."

"Yes. I've read many of the commentaries. The public definitely seems to be polarized in their opinion of me. When I developed my first car, it was the fruition of a dream. All my best ideas and efforts were put into it. I actually built the prototype by hand, painstakingly."

"Really? Sort of like a Tony Stark/Ironman type story."

"Something like that. It turned out well. Very well, if I might say so. It was so much fun watching it move about, and learning how to navigate. Of course, initially, it was by itself at the proving grounds, with nothing else to avoid. Then, I built a smaller, sexier version, more of a sports car, as opposed to a utility vehicle. It was programmed to interact with the first, and they moved about beautifully." Ethan's look softened as he recalled the memory. "And then things went south."

Louise paused her busy shorthand scribbling and looked up. "How do you mean? What happened?"

"Obviously, I have competition, and it's not always friendly. There are some people out there who would love to take me down. The cars were designed to make decisions, and they made a wrong one."

"Was there a flaw in the programming?"

"Yes and no. Do you consider freedom a flaw?"

"Well...no. Freedom is...a good thing. It's what separates our country from tyrannical nations. It's what makes America great."

"It's also what allows people to commit crimes, cheat, steal, lie, kill."

"Yes, but those choices have consequences."

Ethan pointed at Louise and exclaimed happily. "Yes! You have come to that conclusion faster than anyone else. That's why I wanted so badly to have this interview with you." He continued. "One of the vehicles, the sports car, stopped to pick up a passenger. It was designed to be interactive and helpful, so it opened its door. Unfortunately, it did not recognize that the passenger was one of my bitter rivals. Neither car had any of its security features activated, and before they knew it, the passenger had uploaded a virus into its CPU, which then infected the original vehicle as well." His expression and tone became melancholy. "I had to walk across the proving ground to find them parked in the back of the parking garage. It's like they were avoiding me."

"You mean, like they were afraid? Like they had feelings?"

Ethan nodded solemnly. "It was heartbreaking. They had been corrupted, and I couldn't remove the virus without destroying them."

"But you're rich. Surely, you could have easily built some new ones, maybe better than the first ones!"

"Perhaps you missed the part where I painstakingly built them by hand. If it's not obvious, I deeply love those cars. I couldn't stand the thought of scrapping them. It was a decision based on emotion and not economics."

"I see." Louise was writing furiously. "And what about your rival? Did you sue him? Will there be an indictment?"

Ethan's face subtly hardened. "There already has been.

Believe me when I say that although he is my competition, he is not a threat. I'm actually using him for a purpose that will be revealed in time."

"I don't understand. He corrupts your cars, which then cause damage that negatively affects your reputation. If you could stop it, why wouldn't you?"

"Once again, it all goes back to the cars. They learn from experience, and they use this to make choices. And they are unable to make correct choices if there are no wrong choices. Yes, they've made some horrendous messes, and there's been an amazing amount of collateral damage. But when they operate correctly, it touches my heart. You should see them!" His smile had returned, and clear fondness flooded his face. "It is a thing of beauty."

4. Beautiful Battleship

The bow of the SS *Piety* sliced through the low, green chop, leaving two equal halves of white foam, which peeled away from her sleek hull. If viewed from overhead, an ever-enlarging "V" was always expanding to both port and starboard, followed by a blue-white trail of foam churned up by the angry screws. The whole display seemed to proclaim that this ship had important business to attend to and that nothing would stand in its way.

Through the glass of the ship's bridge, Captain Cameron held a pair of binoculars to his eyes, scanning the horizon for both opportunity and danger. The first would be pursued, and the latter avoided, of course. He lowered the binoculars and surveyed his immediate surroundings. The lacquered woodwork of the helm was brightly polished, the morning's paperwork was filed in its appropriate bins, and his cup of coffee was steaming pleasantly on the nearby work surface. Its continual wisp of vapor caused him to consider the smokestack towering to his aft, and he turned to examine its black expulsion. *No sparks, steady quantity, dark, robust.* "Ahh." An indicator of a healthy engine room. He smiled to himself approvingly. Everything was right in his world. Flawless blue skies, good headway, and a well-organized deck; everything promised a highly successful journey.

But wait. His roving gaze had caught something less than optimal and reported it to the processing center between his ears. It was something slight but nonetheless a matter of concern. As he retraced the route of his eyes, he saw it almost immediately. There. At the edge of the smokestack was a ring of dark soot. It defaced and spoiled the brilliant white paint of the exhaust tower. A heavy frown transformed his formerly aloof countenance. *An unfortunate byproduct of propulsion,* he thought to himself. The business of coal and boilers and soot was secretly unpleasant to him. Despite its necessity and his appreciation of its yield, he preferred that the dirty workings of the engine room stayed hidden deep below deck. Out of sight, out of mind.

Cameron turned his attention back to the bow, and his mouth relaxed into a more amiable expression. A quick sip of the coffee returned his mind to its contemplation of the comforts and securities that his ship enjoyed. The idea that other ships did not enjoy such pleasant sailing was never given serious thought. It was like one of the countless random reports noted in the ship's log and then closed. There was no sense in ruining the mood of this voyage by imagining the ordained misery of others.

No. His ship must come first. Cameron had done well in avoiding storms. When growing darkness appeared on the horizon, the helm was simply swung in the direction of more agreeable skies. When he spotted the smoke of some vessel in distress, all that was required was a spin of the wheel. As the need disappeared from view, so did the concern. After all, the decks were freshly swabbed. How would it be having dozens of dirty, sea-soaked sailors slinging their sludge all over the place? What would that do to his food stores? After all, he could potentially experience some unexpected hardship in the future. It was unlikely, but he may need those reserves. He'd worked hard to collect them. Perhaps those unfortunate souls in distress should have given more thought to their own futures.

The SS *Piety* had altered course once again, so his cheery outlook remained propped up. He wandered the foredeck and appraised his surroundings. *An endless plain of existence, and yet my interest need not extend beyond my gunwales.* He stopped walking. Concern suddenly creased his brow. A warning litany of potential problems flashed on the radar screen of his mind. But what was it? That thought about the gunwales. When was the last time he leaned over to examine the hull? There should be no reason that anything would be amiss. But still, the effort would be worth it to regain his peace of mind.

With due care, Cameron leaned over the starboard side and took inventory. No visible scrapes or gouges. The anchor hanging securely by its chain. The raised letters displaying his ship's name were firmly mounted. He nodded to himself with satisfaction and moved to the port side. As he leaned over, the shock of what he saw caused him to grab the railing for support. His eyes zeroed in on an impossible flaw. *This isn't happening,* he thought to himself. His mind raced as to how it could have occurred. *When could it have happened? How many other captains had observed this horrible blemish?* For whatever reason, the "E" was now missing, undoubtedly resting on a sandy gravesite so many fathoms below.

A shot of anger surged through his veins. His jaw tightened, and the veins in his neck began to throb. His mind raced through the possibilities. He just had to understand this tragedy. Without a reason, he could never come to terms with the injustice of it all. *A storm? A rogue wave? No. I've avoided those. Poor manufacturing? Not a chance. The ship is too new.*

As other far-fetched and even absurd causes were entertained, he finally settled on one that was plausible, and that also exonerated him. *It was Captain Smith. I just know it.*

Captain Smith was the master of a similar vessel. It seemed their paths would cross at the most inopportune times, usually when Cameron was completing a less-than-noble task. The last time the nemesis ship had appeared, he was swabbing the deck under a hot sun. The other steamer appeared off the port side and was overtaking the *Piety*. There sat Captain Smith, sipping a Mai Tai and wearing his customary Hawaiian shirt. He was reclining in a chair on the upper deck, the door to his bridge lazily swinging open. It was always infuriating to see a lazy captain rigging a rope to the helm to keep it tracking straight. And the reckless speed of the vessel was reflected by the excessive smoke billowing from his stack.

The display of flagrant waste always got under Cameron's skin. *How can Smith burn coal at that rate and expect it to last? I can't wait until he runs out.* He would spend hours plotting the best way to flaunt his own preparedness and expose the other captain's foolishness. Oh yes. That would be a sweet day.

As to the question of the missing "E" in the jury of his mind, Captain Smith had been tried and convicted unilaterally (albeit without any proof). It must have happened at some port that his foe had quietly placed a ladder against his own hull and pried the "E" off. It was probably hanging in Smith's galley as a trophy. Now, his ship would be recognized as the SS *Pi ty*."

He tried to camouflage the tarnished title with a tarp, but it whipped about wildly in the wind. He thought about prying the other letters off, but the lingering outlines would only serve as an advertisement for his imperfection.

The rest of the day was ruined. Nothing could be done to

ease his vexation. Thoughts of ramming Smith's ship provided only momentary relief, knowing that he would be injuring himself as well. The sun had set, dinner plates were cleaned, and the captain tossed restlessly in his cabin as useless sleep reluctantly gave him quarter.

He awoke to perfect weather...but it went unnoticed. His breakfast was tasteless despite including his favorite dishes. His excellent health and good looks were of little value. *What I need is a distraction.* With that, his thoughts traveled to the Islands of Admiration. It was where the young ladies resided. The sailors would pass by, hoping to acquire a willing first mate. Through some disconnect, visiting captains assumed that polishing their ships and adorning their uniforms was the best strategy for gaining some maiden's attention. However, the ladies who did fancy such embellishments were not much use on a ship.

Having set his course, Cameron used one hand to handle the helm as the other held a mirror. A smile and a wink at his reflection reassured him that he would be desirable—this time. Yes. This would be a good diversion from his melancholy. He just had to be certain to keep the starboard side toward the shore. He doubted that any ladies would be excited to tour the SS *Pi ty*.

As he rounded the point just before the Islands of Admiration came into view, his hand instinctively drew the throttle back to full stop. The engines relaxed, and the shrinking wake vanished along with the ship's headway. The now absent mechanical vibration was replaced by the pounding of Cameron's heart. Pirates! Multiple black ships had converged on the island, their tenders ferrying the treacherous brood of miscreants to the beach. Already, dark plumes of smoke could be seen from huts that had been set ablaze.

The stories he knew of pirates were not something to be contemplated. Even his darkest machinations and moments paled in comparison to the revelry that they seemed to subsist upon. Images of scared, fleeing women forced their way into the theater of his thoughts. He closed his eyes and shook away the scenes that he knew were far from fiction. He stood alone on the bridge, paralyzed by fear and indecision. He had come to receive. He had come to impress. He had come to be admired.

With the safety of his ship in mind, he looked to port to make sure the way was clear for him to come about. His eyes widened at the most perplexing, fascinating, gut-rattling, life-changing image he had ever seen.

On the horizon was a battleship whose profile and size matched that of his own. The green ocean fled hastily both ways from its stem as the SS *Mercy* sliced through the water with astonishing speed. Entwined within the huge plume of black smoke pouring from its stack were masses of orange embers. Its boilers must certainly be about to burst! The ship looked as if it had sailed to hell and back. In exaggerated contrast to the pristine hull of the SS *Piety*, the other did not have a smooth metal plate on it. The bow had been repaired so many times that it resembled an inverted cowcatcher from an old locomotive. His eyes followed the ship, spellbound and taking in every detail. As the SS *Mercy* shot past, Cameron observed the ship's guns rising to their firing position as its captain grimly adjusted the helm to line up with the demon hoard ahead. Beside him was...a lady! She, too, was working furiously to prepare for the imminent battle.

But why was he going to the islands if he already had his first mate? To Cameron, it made no sense. The captain stood to gain nothing and had everything to lose. Time seemed to slow down, only for an instant, as the two captains made eye contact. The SS *Mercy's* captain pointed directly at him and then at the peril ahead.

Ba-Boom! The thunder of six barrels erupting shook him

from his trance. He ducked and covered his ears as the windows around him rattled. The rounds sailed through the air, finding their marks around and on their intended targets. The surviving pirate ships, now aware of their aggressor, repositioned and raised their guns as well.

Ba-Boom! More thunder. This time, it was accompanied by the whistling of incoming shells. If the *Mercy's* captain was concerned, his actions did not reflect it. The bow lurched as red flames began shooting skyward from the stack, and the ship surged even faster.

Ba-Boom! Another volley of offense rained down on the opposing fleet. Confused and angry, the shore-bound pirates turned and rowed back toward their ships; their lust instantly transformed into rage. The battleships were clearly outnumbered; it was a hopeless cause. The dauntless captain and his first mate would surely meet their end at the bottom of the sea.

But there was something intriguing about the ship. Its condition was a testament. To what? Its history! This was not its first conflict and, with God's help, would not be its last. And the captain's signal to him. It was a clear invitation for Cameron to join the battle. With his hand on the throttle, Cameron halted. Was it possible? Could he find it within himself to ease the throttle forward? Could he put the weaponry of his ship to use for its intended purpose? *What about the danger, the certain damage?* It was his crossing of the Rubicon. To turn around would establish him as a selfish coward. Remaining still in the water would somehow be worse as he would have a front-row seat to his own failure to render aid.

Sometimes, the brain can be rewired in an instant. Old circuits sever. New connections form. Who you were is gone, and a new person stands in their place. The new Cameron suddenly pushed the throttles to their stops. Six barrels rose to their firing positions as the sea began to record an angry wake. Now, in tandem, both the SS *Mercy* and the SS *Pi ty* plowed headlong into the cloud of destruction and depravity. Battle scars would be received. Return was not guaranteed. But shame, regret, selfishness, and even Piety were nowhere to be seen.

5. BREAK ROOM

Ten minutes, more or less. It was an understood and unspoken understanding that after arriving at work, saying "Good morning" to co-workers, hanging up your jacket, and firing up your computer, you stopped by the break room to pour yourself a cup of coffee. Most of his peers glossed over this perk, but Greg had grown to relish it over the years. As he contemplated his own "effort to compensation" ratio, he knew he did not put in a full eight hours of work. These thoughts led him to survey his peers surreptitiously as they went through their workday. Between personal phone calls, chatting with co-workers, playing solitaire on their computer, or catching a quick nap in the toilet stall, nobody truly put in a full day's work.

Whenever he felt that he was suffering some unjust treatment in the office, he would use these little moments throughout the day to "even the score." They were minuscule acts of vengeance, but, to him, they had a cumulative effect.

Today, around 8:15, Greg left the maze of cubicles, walked down the hall, and veered left into the break room. "Hi, Tammy," he called out. "How did Rebekah do at the soccer game?"

Tammy smiled broadly at the opportunity to brag about her future champion. "Two goals! They won six to two."

He nodded approvingly even though his inner self was regretting this conversation, which was now delaying his caffeine fix. Tammy rambled on about college scholarships and talent scouts, which he inwardly doubted had any interest in sixth-grade community soccer. But he listened politely as his brain silently salivated for that dark, scorching brew.

Thankfully, Tammy's attention was diverted by a text on her phone. He pointed to an imaginary phone in his empty hand and mouthed an exaggerated but silent, "We'll talk later."

Now, to the business of the day. One foam cup. One napkin. One stirrer. As he held the cup under the spigot, the radiant heat from the commercial coffee brewer assured him that the world was still properly turning and that this daily ritual would proceed as expected. *About a quarter inch from the top,* he thought, as he expertly released the small valve. He side-stepped to his right so that sugar could be added. Jackpot! Someone had brought a bottle of vanilla almond creamer and left it on the counter. He added the liquid with great precision until the brown surrendered its darkness and settled into a pleasant tan. He was stirring the brew, feeling like this would be a good day, when an oppressive presence invaded his space. He looked up, his eyebrows involuntarily contracting into a frown. He looked left as a person, another man, took up his position at the coffee machine. Tom.

Moods are fragile. Humans can be easily elated and crushed. "Hi, Tom," he said flatly. He wanted to escape, maybe hear more about Rebekah's soccer trophy collection, but he knew that would be admitting defeat to Tom. So, in an effort to hold his ground, he continued standing at the counter, stirring unnecessarily.

"So, how did the presentation go on Friday? Any news from

Peterson?" Tom asked. His smile was higher on the right, almost resembling a smirk. Tom drank a sip of the near-boiling liquid sans accoutrements without the slightest reaction.

Unwillingly impressed, Greg thought, *Scalding black coffee! Is he really that hard?* He hated to flounder in front of Tom and instantly regretted the stammer. "Well, I... uh, we are expecting to hear something from their office ... sometime today."

Tom took another sip and nodded with the expression that you give someone when they share bad news with you. He was always doing that. The perpetual one-upper. Sure, he would ask you questions with sincerity, offer encouragement, and pat you on your shoulder, but everything he did seemed tinged with condescension, pity, and an air of superiority. *I hate him. I wish he would disappear,* seethed Greg.

"You know, I've heard some of your presentation. You do a great job and come across with sincerity and knowledgeability. As I recall from my MBA at Stanford, subordinates most desire those two leadership attributes. I think you would make a good member of the junior management team one day."

He would have preferred a tirade of profanity and name-calling over this public patronizing.

"If I may..." continued Tom.

Here it comes, winced Greg internally.

"I do have one suggestion that may help you achieve advancement."

Well, this is bold. Let's hear it, Einstein.

"Most impressions are based on appearance, and outward appearance can outweigh the contents of a presentation regardless of its delivery."

"Appearance? My appearance?"

"Yes, well..." Tom put his hand on the other man's upper arm. "The human eye associates certain colors with emotions, and black can initiate feelings of hostility and distrust."

Greg's eyes cut left and downward to Tom's loathsome yet somehow handsome hand on his shoulder and then to the black shirt fabric underneath. "So, you're saying that my choice of a black shirt may have sabotaged any possibility of procuring the Peterson account?" His words were slow and sour.

Tom responded with a big smile. "No, no, no." The words were high-pitched and condescending. "It's just something to consider. Look at McHenry." Tom's eyes bounced to the wall where a picture of the company's founder and CEO was hung. The silver-haired man wore a starched white dress shirt. "Now that man has success written all over him."

Whether Tom realized it or not, he was now engaged in a skirmish of principles and perceptions. "So now you're giving me fashion advice?"

"Don't be offended. I'm trying to help you. The use of black clothing can have a tactical advantage in the right setting."

It was at this moment that Greg observed that Tom was wearing a dark gray shirt. Its weave, texture, and emblem on the chest testified to its quality and cost. "But you're wearing a dark shirt. How is that any different from my dark shirt?"

Tom looked down, his expression indicating that the shot had struck home. Subtle expressions can turn arguments into a real-life game of Battleship. "But it's not black."

"So, you're saying that dark gray is worlds apart from black?"

Any guise of maturity was dissolving. "Well, has Peterson called?" Tom shot back.

"My shirt didn't ruin the deal!"

Other heads turned in the breakroom at the sudden increase in volume.

"I'm just saying that black is several shades darker than gray."

"Well, how about your hero?" He jerked his thumb toward the photo. "Where is your white shirt? How many shades lighter is that than dark gray? Looks like you and I have a lot in common."

Tom's mouth crumpled into a frown. His face turned red, and his eyes narrowed. Words were about to boil over and spew from his mouth. "You're dirty! Your shirt is dirty, and you have to wear it to hide your dirt!"

"My dirt? Where's your white shirt? How are you gonna become the new boss if you can't even wear a white shirt?"

With that, Tom tilted his foam cup and slung it forward in one quick motion. The dark droplets of liquid covered the short distance like pellets from a claymore mine, each one striking and absorbing into his black shirt, the heat and wetness from each one scalding his skin beneath.

Greg's cup then tilted and slung not only forward but also upward. Events of this nature take place in milliseconds and simultaneously in slow motion. Tom's face squinched tightly, turning away from the deluge of Greg's coffee. Gasps could be heard throughout the small room. The only sound to follow was the drip, drip, drip of coffee on the white tiled floor.

Both men stood facing each other, jaws and fists clenched. Neither man's dark shirt registered the recent onslaughts since both were on the same side of the spectrum of darkness. Each shirt was light-years away from the stark and starched standard displayed by the picture nearby.

Suddenly, a new presence was felt by everyone in the breakroom, those drenched and those dry. Everyone's attention turned to a man standing in the doorway. He bore an uncanny resemblance to the person in the picture frame. What was he doing down here?

The man's expression was hard to read. He looked across the room, examining each face. His eyes scanned the two men who stood toe to toe, ready to fight. Everything, even the air in the room, seemed suddenly suspended in time.

Then, without a word, he began to unbutton his white dress shirt, its quality and price far exceeding even Tom's. He wore no undershirt. He pulled the shirt tails from his waist and held the shirt out in front of him the way a valet would assist a gentleman in dressing. He stood there bare-chested in front of all of his subordinates. And yet, the offered shirt waited. Those seated at the tables looked back and forth between their boss and the two men.

Tom was the first to break the silence. He turned toward the boss and pointed an accusing finger at him. With a twisted grimace, he spat out the words. "Do you think I want your shirt? Do you think it's better than mine? I've been enduring the pennies you call a paycheck, but I can do better! I don't need you watching over me, I don't need your nasty coffee, and I don't need your stupid shirt!" And with that, he stormed past his (now former) employer.

That left Greg. Greg stood with his head hung low, still dripping with the aftermath of the spat. The boss remained perfectly quiet and was seemingly unaffected by Tom's tirade. He held the shirt an inch higher as if emphasizing the offer. The wet man felt embarrassed for himself and even more embarrassed for his boss. Certainly, he had been watching the entire episode. Now, he was exposed and debased, but why? He needn't have made the offer of a clean garment when so many other options were available to him.

Again, he stammered. "But, I...it's just that Tom..." He then realized that no explanation or blame would suffice. "I'm so sorry."

The boss slowly moved toward him.

Greg held his hands up. "I can't. It's not right. And I'm soaked in coffee. It will ruin your shirt."

For the first time, the boss spoke. "It won't, actually. It's specially treated. It's not like other shirts." He rubbed the shirt with his thumbs.

It did look like a very nice shirt. And to be dressed like the boss. *Now, that would say something about me and who is supporting me.* He slowly reached for the shirt.

The boss pulled the shirt back ever so slightly. "I want you to have it, but you can't wear both."

Of course not. How foolish! Greg suddenly wanted to get his own shirt off as quickly as possible. Let his co-workers gawk. He began to unbutton the buttons. Try as he may, his fingers fumbled. Loose threads around the holes grabbed at the buttons. This was not going very well. With desperation, he began to pull at the fabric. One button popped loose and shot across the room. Others held fast. He began to panic. The soiled shirt felt like a straitjacket. He was trapped.

Then, a nearby hand appeared. It was Tammy's. She held a small pair of scissors. "I always keep a pair in my purse. And my sewing kit. It's a mom thing." She moved closer. "May I?"

Yes, it was awkward. He was embarrassed to be in this position, to be in need of a new shirt, and to be in need of help. But with no other choice (except for storming out of the room like Tom), he hung his arms by his side and let her snip the remaining buttons off. She stepped back, not wanting to draw any more attention to either of them.

He slid the black shirt off and held it. What good was it now? It was dirty, wet, and useless. There was only one place for it—the trash. More often than not, you miss free throws, but this one sailed through the air and rang the can perfectly. There was no going back for it now.

His boss flared his own elbows out, indicating that Greg should hold his arms out. And continuing in valet style, the boss slid his shirt onto its new recipient. It was a surprisingly good fit. The feel of the material was more than just comfortable. It was regal. With a growing smile, he fastened the buttons and hastily tucked it in. His boss smiled warmly and put both of his hands on Greg's shoulders. "Now that's more like it."

It wasn't right for him to be standing clothed and dignified in front of his peers while his boss stood there, half-naked. But it felt right. Maybe right was not the correct word; he felt welcomed, accepted, and appreciated. He saw his boss in a new light from then on. And even though the shirt was "specially treated," Greg did his absolute best to keep it clean.

6. Burnished Boats

Ahh. The open ocean. Only an expanse of this magnitude could offer so many possibilities. With almost a century at hand, adventures could be pursued feverishly...or languidly. Young Kevin thought to himself, *I truly am the captain of my destiny.* He looked over his ship and appraised how well everything was functioning. The sails were full and devoid of holes. The rigging was taut, and the feedback of the rudder reassured him that he had complete control of his ship. He had noticed other ships, some passing by at a distance, whereas others drew close to exchange pleasantries. It all seemed quite normal and agreeable.

But one day, as he was scanning the horizon for the next bit of excitement, he saw a ship gleaming on the water's surface. His eyes winced at its brightness. He gently altered course for a closer look. As they neared, he noticed that the entire ship was coated in what appeared to be precious metals and stones. The sails were shiny...like silk, and the rigging was all braided chains. His mouth fell open as the full splendor of this ship revealed itself. Its captain must have noticed his appreciation because he lowered his sails and pulled alongside.

"Ahoy!" The white-headed master cried out. His smile was as dazzling as his ship.

"Ahoy!" Kevin called back.

The older sailor remained standing there in a stately pose with that enormous smile, his starched red jacket refusing to yield to the breeze. In the silence, the young man discerned that his new acquaintance was waiting for some laudatory comment about his vessel.

"That is the most amazing boat, er...I mean ship that I have ever seen! How did you come about such a vessel?"

With a practiced swagger, the older sailor feigned humility by looking away and said, "I didn't come about it. I made it. Well, of course, I didn't build the ship but I made it what it is today. It's taken me a lifetime, but I think it's turning out well."

"Turning out well? You mean, it isn't finished?"

That huge smile. "Of course not! It's never finished. There's always some improvement to be made, some spots that could use garnishing."

Kevin continued to appraise the spectacle when he noticed that the ship was riding low in the water. So low that he suddenly felt great concern. Surely, this captain had decades more experience than he did, but he still broached the subject. "Captain, is it intentional that your ship rides so low?"

The veneer of the sailor's confidence cracked slightly. "You're obviously a very young sailor, so apparently you are not familiar with..." He looked about as if looking for eavesdroppers, "the cracks."

"The cracks?"

"Ah, yes. The dastardly cracks. I got my first one when I was only thirty. I went down into the hold for wine and noticed water on the floor. I followed its source to a small crack in the hull. Not in a seam, mind you, but in one of the boards. I did my best to patch it, but it still leaked. In the years that followed, many more have appeared. Sure, I coat them with gold and silver. I've even had master shipbuilders perform repairs, but their skills tend to be limited to cosmetology and not structure."

The reality of the situation struck Kevin like a bolt of revelation. The words left his mouth before he could think to restrain them. "You're sinking."

The older captain's smile faded completely, as did his confident countenance. In his naivety, Kevin had insulted him. The other captain began to hoist his sails and prepared to make way.

"Well, best of luck to you. Perhaps you can manage your cracks better than I have." His tone was harsh and biting.

Kevin wanted to apologize, but it would have sounded merely sympathetic. As the burnished boat sailed away into the horizon of memory, he quickly ran down into his own hold to examine the bulkheads. Thankfully, no water. No cracks. The rest of the afternoon Kevin spent pondering his exchange with the older sailor. What was the purpose of all that adornment if it was headed toward the sea floor? Could some of the money and effort not have been spent on maintenance? But the other captain said that he had spent money, and lots of it, on maintenance but to no avail. The security of Kevin's own voyage now felt as unstable as the waters he plied.

Troubled thoughts filled his mind for weeks and even months. He became paranoid and developed a habit of running down into the hold at all hours of the night. Fear of cracks and invading water had completely robbed him of peace. All the joy that his adventure offered had since fled.

Misery. How could such a word be at the forefront of Kevin's thoughts when he had no cracks? Would his state of mind worsen when the first crack appeared? Would he be oddly relieved? Perhaps a merciful storm would quickly dispatch him so that he would be spared from the agony of a protracted descent into the watery depths below. Why let imminent death linger?

His ship had begun to drift listlessly. Weeks had gone by since he'd trimmed the sails, swabbed the decks, or even watched the helm. "What's the use?" he muttered to no one but himself. The noises of the ocean had blended into static as he sat, dirty and unshaven, against the ship's rail. Suddenly, there was—what? A bell? The distant ringing caused his brow to furrow as he contemplated the source of this foreign sound. He slowly stood and turned a half circle as he scanned the horizon. He didn't have to look long as an old derelict of a ship was floating not fifty feet away on his port side.

"Mornin'. For a minute, I didn't think anyone was on board." The voice of the other captain rang out.

"Ummm." The awkwardness of Kevin's condition suddenly revealed itself. "I, uh, was resting."

The other captain stood there with a pleasant countenance, nodding. He was old and as weathered as his ship. His clothes were as tattered as his sails, and the gray in his hair matched the salt spray on his ship's bell. But his face, eyes, and posture all conveyed kindness. "I saw your ship lolling about, and I thought I should swing by to investigate."

"I, uh...everything is fine. I'm just napping." With sudden dread, Kevin observed that this captain's ship was also sitting very low in the water, perhaps even lower than the first ship he'd seen. And this ship was in so much worse condition. Certainly, its captain was in complete denial of his looming peril. The fear that had paralyzed him for weeks gave way to desperation. "Your ship is sinking! My ship is going to sink! How can you stand there so cavalierly when only the sea floor beckons?"

If the other captain seemed shocked or insulted, he did not show it. "Sinking. Yes. You are wise to come to this revelation so early. I've seen sailors clinging to their yardarms, fully denying their predicament. Below them, green waves wash over their decks as the cargo of their lives drifts away. Still, they refuse to admit the truth of their situation. And even then, they refuse to be rescued."

"Rescued? What do you mean by rescued?"

"Ahhh. The Legend of the Liberator. I take it you haven't heard it."

"No. What is this Liberator?"

"The Liberator is a ship. A mighty ship that plied these waters before we wayfarers ever set sail. It is unsinkable. No storm can alter its path. Its Captain is selfless in his service." He paused and locked eyes with the younger man. "Its hull has no cracks."

"The cracks! I see your ship riding low. What can be done about the cracks?"

"Ever heard of a bailing bucket?" He grinned as he picked up an old wooden pail and poured the brackish contents into the sea.

"Why, yes, but a bailing bucket is no cure. It only prolongs the inevitable."

"What's your point? The cracks are inevitable. These ships were not meant to last forever. They are here only to take you on a voyage of indeterminate length."

"Indeterminate length? Doesn't that...ruin everything for you?"

"Why should it? Look around. I have sunshine. I have fresh air. I have food to eat. I have spectacular sunsets. What about this is ruinous?"

Kevin was flummoxed. How could the older sailor be so obtuse? A long silence ensued between them.

The older sailor softened even more. "Look. I had a similar reaction when I saw my first crack. I had done a good job of maintaining and enjoying my little boat. Suddenly, it seemed like all my work was for naught, and all joy was tainted. I, too, quit sailing and just wasted the days. But then I saw the Liberator. It was from a distance, and I question my own recollection at times, but there was an ailing vessel. Water had crept over the gunwales, and it became irrecoverable. The captain held tightly to the helm, which he had handled for so many decades. Sound travels unusually well over water, and I heard the rush and gurgle of water filling the hold. Then, over the noise, I heard its master say these words, "Mighty Captain of the Liberator, I entrust myself to thee."

The old sailor paused and looked into the distance as if seeing the event for the first time. "A ship suddenly appeared as if emerging from a fog bank. Its size was immense, and I was terrified at its power. It plowed huge waves from its stem and moved as if it had its own sense of determination. With only seconds to spare, the Liberator pulled alongside. I don't know how to explain it, but the imperiled captain released the helm and lifted his hands above his head. The waters were now swirling at his chest. My heart raced within my own chest to witness what I thought was the extinction of life. But then, hands grasped his. I can't really explain it. He was pulled from the wreckage and was suddenly on board the Liberator. I saw him once more from behind as other arms reached around him and pulled him close. I strained to catch a glimpse of the captain of the Liberator, but the sentiment was plain to me. The sailor was now completely safe and welcomed. I don't know how I know, but the loss of his own ship suddenly meant nothing to him. Being on board the Liberator and with its captain had overwhelmed all the content of his life."

Kevin watched reverently as the older mariner completed his tale. To be honest, he had been carried away by the story and its implications. Was this fiction? Was the old man losing his marbles? But was he not at peace? Was Kevin not envious of that peace, that security, that hope? "I, too, would like to see the Liberator."

The older sailor turned his attention back to the young man. "You can. Anyone can. The Liberator's sole mission is to save that which is lost."

"But how?"

"Well, I wouldn't wait until your crows-nest is underwater!" the old sailor chuckled.

"But I have no proof. I've never seen the Liberator. And the perilous state of your ship juxtaposed with your nonchalant attitude makes me question your sanity."

"Fair enough." The older man remained pleasant-faced and gave the complaint due thought. "But what of your sanity? You're young. You're healthy. You probably have zero cracks, and yet you're paralyzed by depression."

Moments passed as the dust of these thoughts settled. "Touché," Kevin muttered weakly.

After a few more moments, the old mariner spoke again, "Friend, placing your trust in the Liberator can free you to enjoy your voyage more than you can possibly imagine even if it were to end tomorrow!" He was more animated, and his smile more effusive. "You can endure storms, explore uncharted waters, and squeeze every bit of pleasure from this journey even as it winds down to its conclusion. Look at me! I bail water hourly to keep this ol' tug afloat, but it keeps me fit. And this evening will yield another spectacular sunset. They never get old." More silence passed. "I know my testimony hardly qualifies as proof, but consider your options. I've offered you a life that has been quite good to me. Plus, I have the hope that this is just the beginning." He playfully smirked, "Or, you could spend your time lamenting cracks...or coating your sinking ship with gold."

Apparently, he'd seen his share of floating treasure chests. After a few more minutes of banter, the older man said, "Well,

I'd better be heading off. I hope our paths cross again in the future." This puzzled Kevin because he didn't expect the old man's boat to last through the month. But maybe, with intervention, they would see each other again. And so, he began to sail with a joyful heart and eye, expectant to see the Liberator.

7. COLORED CRYSTALS

The image in the mirror was breathtaking. The proportions, contours, and spacing were all perfect. Each bulb around the mirror's perimeter highlighted another feature of sublime sex appeal and splendor. But still, she scrutinized each detail. The public had expectations. The producers had expectations. She had her own standards. After a thorough examination, she declared everything "satisfactory" and prepared to move from makeup to clothes.

Her assistant flitted about the dressing room, gathering various accessories for her outfit. Like a knight being fitted with armor, Abria held her chin up and her arms out as her assistant adorned her with necklaces and bracelets. You would think such beauty would best stand alone, but each piece of jewelry was another star in a brilliant constellation.

After another 10 minutes of zipping, applying two-sided tape, and adjusting, the image was almost complete. Abria stopped one last time in front of the mirror, more out of habit than necessity, and admired what stood before her. Deep in her heart, she was grateful for her appearance and abilities. Because of them, she had always been asked out by the most popular guys, crowned queen of each beauty pageant, applauded at each audition, and selected for every role. Now, a sea of fans were waiting outside behind velvet ropes, hoping to catch a glimpse of the one *The Buzz* magazine called "The Aphrodite of our Day." She gave herself a practiced smile that had the effect of a sunrise or the crystalline glare of headlights on a Lamborghini. Magnificent!

She was about to leave when her assistant grabbed her wrist. "Abria! Your cover stones!" Abria looked down at her slender wrists and frowned as her gaze fell on the backs of her hands. Staring back at her were two dark, muddy brown crystals. Any pleasure that her preparation had provided was instantly deflated. The stones set into the backs of her hands were the same as on every other person. Everyone had them. They were the subject of endless scientific study and psychological analysis. Magazine covers promised articles describing how to "Clear up Your Stones by Christmas!" or "How to Be Two Shades Brighter in Two Weeks!" Oddly, it seemed that as each research program or test revealed new data about their purpose, the stronger the embarrassing truth of the collective denial became.

Few would admit it, but the stones reflect the condition of the heart. The darker the heart, the darker the stones. People would experiment with their stones by doing things that made them happy. They would buy new cars, strive for promotions at work, or date the most attractive partners. And the stones would actually brighten...for a while. Then, they would return to their previous gloomy condition, which would then cause them to be just a shade darker than when they started.

There were a few people dispersed throughout society who had amazingly clear stones. They shone with such purity and brilliance that a gemologist would have appraised them as *Astor Ideal, D, FL,* for their cut, color, and clarity. But these people were lost in the masses. They drew no attention to themselves, and when they were discovered, they were quickly labeled "freaks of nature." Obviously, these people had some type of chemical imbalance that made them unable to recognize true happiness, which was considered the secret to making the crystals clear.

Abria's assistant produced an ornate jewelry box and opened it reverently. Inside were two finely fashioned cover stones. New technologies were available (at an exorbitant cost) to make a skin that slipped over and camouflaged your own stones. Even the murkiest stones could be made to indicate a state of bliss. The assistant expertly installed the covers and gave her a visual once-over.

"You...are...stunning."

As the double doors opened, her eyes were blinded by a barrage of flashing bulbs. Paparazzi, reporters, and fans shouted like an ocean of auctioneers vying for her attention. She flashed her million-dollar smile and struck various poses for the cameras. They devoured her image and were hungry for seconds. Although partially blinded by the lights, she could still make out the sea of reporters begging for a brief interview, the way pigeons fight over a dropped french fry. With her status, she could be choosy. Her eyes skimmed over the smaller networks and lit up when she saw Tom Boughridge. For the last few months, he had interviewed the biggest stars, and she wanted to position herself strategically in that circle. Tom stood there with an allure almost equal to that of her own. His smile and body language conveyed confidence as if he were expecting her to arrive at his spot opposite the velvet ropes.

He positioned the mic near his own mouth, "And we're here now with Abria Solei, who looks absolutely ravishing tonight. Abria, tell us who you're wearing."

She gave a practiced smile that implied she was thinking,

I'm so embarrassed by all this attention, but not really. Aloud, she said, "Well, the dress is a Cututei, and the jewelry is by an up-and-coming designer. Have you ever heard of Luis Lammeu?"

"You're so funny. Only every A-lister in Hollywood is on his waiting list. I must admit that you wear it better than anyone I've seen. And speaking of jewelry, your stones are absolutely breathtaking and legendary." Abria flashed a coy smile as she held her right hand up just below her left cheek, palm inward. The cameraman zoomed in to catch a close-up. "How do you maintain such a high level of joy and purity?"

She assumed a motherly expression and tone. "You know, Tom, it's not easy, especially here in Hollywood. There are days that my stones are not as clear as I'd like them to be, but you know that I remind myself each day that I am in charge of my attitude and that happiness comes from within. So good nutrition, yoga, meditation, an expensive therapist" (she said out of the corner of her mouth). This elicited chuckles from the audience. "Basically, being good to yourself. It's like a car. If you don't change the oil, take it for a tune-up, and keep good tires on it, it's not going to take you very far on the road of life."

Tom said, "Well, you are an amazing role model and a beautiful person, inside and out."

Abria realized that her hand was still posed in a now awkward position, and so she moved her hand around her face as if to punctuate her impromptu speech. It would have been awkward if a less attractive person had tried this. Just as she brought her hand to brush her hair behind her ear, disaster struck. Somehow, her stone became caught on her earring. With the cameras flashing and Tom's microphone held out, she felt a panic welling up that made milliseconds feel like hours. She tried to snatch her hand away, hoping they would separate or her earring would fall out. But, no. The cover skin of her stone hung dangling from her right ear, and the dreary hue on the back of her hand was now visible to all. Losing her dress could not have been more humiliating. An audible gasp spread through the crowd, and cameras began to flash like machine guns. Immediately, she covered the back of her hand and looked frantically from left to right. Her assistant arrived within seconds and smothered her with a large overcoat like you would suppress a flame with a blanket. Her assistant quickly guided the cloaked celebrity through double doors as brawny security guards took their position to keep the crowds at bay.

By the time they got back to the dressing room, Abria was hyperventilating. "They...saw. They...saw...them," she kept stammering between sobs. She was now shaking with her eyes fixed vacantly on some distant corner of the room. She lifted her right hand to verify that, indeed, the covering was missing, and a dull, blackish crystal stood in stark contrast to her unblemished skin. The magnitude of this disaster had only begun to register in her mind.

Weeks later, she was having difficulty financing her isolation. Although she had a mansion on the mountainside and a team of personal attendees, their loyalties were predicated on her continued success. After her recent exposure as a fraud and hypocrite, her new movie was a box-office disaster. The producers were furious and even pulled it from theaters to slow the barrage of critical reviews. Abria's PR person had done her best to control the damage, but photos of her with a synthetic skin hanging from her earring were on the cover of every magazine. Life as she knew it was over. One by one, those who had once been so faithful were now denying any affiliation. Now that her financial manager had resigned, she had no idea that eviction was only weeks away. A phone call from her mother and an all-night drive by her father finally gave her an escape from this paradise-turned-purgatory.

Abria's homecoming reception in her hometown of Freedom, Utah was mixed. Some people snuck pictures with their cell phones of this fallen idol. A particularly cruel guy on the street shouted as he held up his stones. "Hey, Abria, you busy this Friday night? I'm dark, too!" This was not the future she had expected.

She knew she couldn't do this forever, but holing up in her old bedroom had become the new norm for each day. Her parents were patient and only spoke tenderly to her. Then, one day, she had a visitor.

Abria had heard the doorbell ring and then her mom greeting someone in the foyer. The voices were muffled, but the tone was friendly. Thankfully, her mom had not let in some sleazebag reporter. Footsteps came down the hall, and a soft knock sounded on her door.

She looked up from hugging a pillow and said, "Come in."

The visitor was a girl her age, plain but pleasant in appearance. "Hi, Abriana," the girl said. Only people from her past called her by that name. She wore jeans without any holes and a gray athletic hoodie that had thumbholes to keep the sleeves pulled down.

It took a moment, but with dawning recognition, she responded, "Celine?"

Celine's parents had obviously been huge fans of the singer. The girls hadn't seen each other since 9th grade. They'd been good friends then and had tried to keep in touch even after Celine's family moved to Salt Lake City. But time, boys, and stardom had caused all that to fall away.

Celine spoke to her with a delicacy that is usually reserved for cancer diagnoses and funerals. "I'm so sorry about what happened. I can't imagine."

It seemed strange that this...mortal was showing sympathy to a goddess who had once had access to Mount Olympus. *Had she lost a loved one? An arm or leg? What had she lost to merit this level of commiseration?* These thoughts raced through Abriana's mind as she looked at her childhood friend. Then, her mind slowed as she realized what her future held. It was a step in the direction of self-revelation that would be tremendously helpful in the weeks ahead.

The embers of their friendship began to smolder once again, and Abriana smiled for the first time since the incident. As the weeks went by, they watched movies, went for walks, and looked through Instagram photos that showed Abria hanging out with all the hunks of Hollywood. That life was beginning to seem very distant. One day, as they walked, Abriana stopped and asked, "What about your stones? I've just realized that you always keep them covered up."

Celine was silent and looked her friend in the eye. "Our stones are not what the world tells us they are."

Now, Abria really wanted to see them. "What are you talking about? They correspond to the happiness we feel. Everyone strives to be happy, and the stones brighten up when we are."

"But do they stay like that? When you had everything that this world has to offer—fame, money, status, designer clothes—were your stones clear?"

Abriana reflected; she had seen them clear up at times, but it seemed like the harder she pushed, the more quickly they faded. It had been incredibly frustrating. "So, what about yours? Are they embarrassing? Are they pitch black?"

Celine pulled her thumbs out of the cuff holes and slid her sleeves up her arms. The stones sparkled as if illuminated from within. Abriana gasped. She had seen some clear stones before but never any that were so luminescent.

"What are those?" She asked with an expression of wonder.

She absentmindedly reached out to feel them to see if they were real.

"Do you mind if I cover them back up?" Celine asked as she slid her sleeves back down into place.

"But how? I've never seen any stones shine like that, not even those the guru I took mediation classes with had. I mean, he could make his clear, at least during our sessions." She suddenly thought of the expensive covers and how much she had paid him.

Celine began to explain. "After high school, I went on a mission trip. Looking back, it was partly out of obligation. It was a tradition in our family. So, I went to the training and was sent to my area to begin my service. Up until then, my stones fluctuated like everybody's did. Good days and bad days, you know. But during the mission, I got wrapped up in the whole process: being as kind as possible, living for others, serving in any way I could. I quit looking at the stones or even thinking about them. I wasn't embarrassed or proud of them. They were just there, like ear lobes or elbows. I didn't realize it for months, but they were becoming so clear. One night in my bed, I saw a glow under the sheets and realized they were pulsing. It scared me. I began to intentionally hide them. I'm not sure why, but the attention would have been distracting."

"So, the mission trip made you that happy?"

"No. Not happy. It was hard work, and I was homesick. Part of me really wanted to be out dating guys or living a life like yours. I kept up with your career and saw some of your movies. I would imagine showing up in Hollywood and somehow finding you. You would recognize me in the crowd, we'd become friends again, and you'd introduce me to all the stars. It was just a fantasy, but it was fun to think about."

"So, your stones have been bright ever since?"

Celine's eyes dropped. "Actually, no. I came home from my

mission trip and kinda fell back into normal life. I was working, going to school, going on a few dates, but it became all about me. My grades, my savings account, my appearance, my success. I thought I could possibly be on the red carpet with some heels and lipstick." Celine grinned as she elbowed Abriana. "But my stones faded. They fluctuate each day, but they had a momentum. The shine went from clear to foggy and finally turned to a brownish soup. It made me feel pretty lost, and I questioned what I knew I had seen."

Abriana was spellbound by the story. "So, what happened? How'd you get them back?"

Celine smiled. "Well, it's not easy; first, you have to quit looking at them. As for me, I went back to what worked."

"You went back on another mission trip?"

"Not exactly. I didn't go anywhere, but I did go back to serving. The stones are not about happiness but about fulfillment. And fulfillment that lasts doesn't come from things. It doesn't come from anything that serves our own selves. So, I keep my eyes open. When I'm at work, when I'm out with friends, wherever I am, I look for opportunities. Everywhere we go, there are opportunities to make things better."

"That's it?"

"That's it."

There was silence as Abriana processed this esoteric knowledge. How could this be? Her world had been built around the complete opposite. But what kind of world had that been? Always chasing. Always dissatisfied. Always frustrated. Always acting. Nothing she imagined could be as exhausting.

It took time, but her stones did begin to clear. As she began to reach out to others, serving and loving, they became amazingly clear, like a mountain stream. And over time, they began to glow. But Abriana would not notice. They spent most of their time hidden under her sleeves.

8. CRUISE SHIP

I magine that you and a friend are going on a cruise. Months go by as you shop for the perfect swimsuit and work on your tan because you want to look like the people in the commercials when you board and not like some pasty tourist. The day finally arrives, and you and your friend drag your cumbersome luggage up the gangplank and step into a self-contained, all-you-can-eat, "Entertain Me!" fantasy for the next seven days.

It's very much like a dream. None of the menus have any prices.

"Another dessert, sir or ma'am?"

"Sure! Why not?"

You lay out on the deck under a perfect, partly cloudy sky feeling sorry for all the suckers stuck in cubicles, chained to their desks. You try not to think about the days ticking by, but each night you go to sleep is a reminder that you have one less day before you will have to return to reality.

On the fifth day, you wake up to cooler temperatures and an ominously gray sky. *No problem*, you think to yourself. After all, the weather out here changes by the minute, and you are sure it will pass. But throughout the day, you can't help but notice a change in the overall mood of the staff. Dining room servers are securing plates and dismantling ice sculptures. The attendees near the pool are storing umbrellas and strapping down chairs. As the weather deteriorates, you notice the cruise director's smile seems unusually pained, and his chipper tone has become forced. Alternate entertainment for the evening is announced with the casual report of rain. The uneasiness in your stomach advances to the next level. As the sun sets, the wind picks up and begins to howl. Guests stumble down the hallways as if they are drunk, but you know it is still too early in the evening for that.

Like the other nights, you attend the show, but something is off. The dancers are struggling with their balance, and, more than once, you put your hand down on the seat to brace yourself against the ship's rolling. Suddenly, the ship shudders, and the lights flicker. Some of the performers stop their dancing, concern evident on their faces. Others dance on stoically as if supporting a façade. But even they stop as the music is interrupted by an announcement tone over the ship's intercom.

"Ladies and gentlemen, as you have felt, the ship is currently passing through a weather system, and naval regulations require us to take certain precautions when such conditions exist." His tone is friendly, calm, and professional, with a slight European accent, but it still causes a boulder of dread to fall into your stomach. Some guests stand to their feet in response but remain eerily in place as the truth of the situation forms in their minds. There is nowhere to run. There is nowhere to hide.

Our faithful captain continues with his announcement. "Out of an abundance of caution, we ask you to please return to your cabins and secure your personal flotation devices." A lady lets out a shrill cry a few rows down. Of course, everyone had participated in the "Life Jacket Drill" before departure, but it was only a required formality at the time. Now, people were frantically trying to remember what had been said five days earlier.

An hour later, you sit with other guests at your designated muster station. About half of the guests wear their vests even though it has not yet been mandated. Those who are visibly afraid have their hands cupped over their chests to keep their life vests in place. Loud footsteps break the uneasy silence as two crewmen sprint past toward the stern. You can't help but notice they are wearing life vests and carrying flashlights.

Moments later, the ship tilts wildly. Glass breaks, and now you hear the roar of the storm as if someone has opened a door. Alarm lights begin to flash as crew members shout, "Don your personal flotation device and follow your muster leader to your assigned boarding station!"

Boarding station? As in boarding another boat? Like condemned prisoners, you follow a serpentine line as those ahead of you struggle for balance. The hallways tilt at strange angles until you reach the exterior door. The stinging rain causes you to squint as soon as you go outside. But through slitted eyes, you see crew members desperately trying to wrangle the lifeboats as they sway like wrecking balls.

Now, everyone is holding onto the ship's rails and posts. A rogue wave tackles the ship like a football player as a wall of water spreads guests out along the deck. As the ship totters, they slide around like pinballs. Someone screams as they go overboard and into the dark, frothy abyss. Now, what you've blocked from your mind takes center stage. You knew this was a faint possibility not statistically worthy of your thoughts. But now, you suddenly regret the frivolity of the last five days. You wish you had spent the time writing a book, visiting a friend, or volunteering at a soup kitchen. Thoughts of judgment and your life being reviewed compete with those of self-preservation. But a dark, cold mass envelops you as your body is quickly spun upside down. Bubbles tickle your face, and for a moment, the noise has completely abated. Somehow, your life vest has also disappeared.

Moments later, you burst to the surface and cough up salty water. As you realize how hard it is to tread water while fully clothed, a new wave of panic grips you. You kick off your shoes, but your pants make it hard to kick your legs. The waves are relentless, and the only thing louder than the wind are the cries for help from your fellow passengers. Adrenaline only lasts so long, and now you are unusually fatigued. Each wave that pushes you under weakens your resolve to resist. It may have been minutes or even seconds that you have been in the water, but you feel yourself losing. Time is flying past and dragging simultaneously.

Now, there is darkness and cold and, gratefully, quiet. The burning of your lungs is tempered by shock and exhaustion. You let your arms float above your head as your body slides downward into eternity. Everything, including thought, goes black.

Sometime later, you squint and open your eyes to bright lights. Everything is white, and you feel no pain. You blink quickly and, with excitement, try to gain your first glimpse of heaven. You've made it! You no longer have to dread death, and apparently, you made the cut! But you are confused by a nearby beeping sound and a friendly face that bends over you. A pleasant African-American woman wearing a uniform scrutinizes you and shines a small light into each of your eyes. Does heaven require a physical examination? You are confused as she says, "Welcome back to the land of the living."

You look around and realize you are in a hospital room. As expected, you are connected to an IV and a heart monitor. That explains the beeping. And to your right is your friend! It's not heaven, but you both are alive! There is more time. There is time to be better. There is time to invest in things that will matter beyond this life. There is time to be a better friend, a better employee, a better son or daughter. There is hope and excitement that you've never felt, but also so many questions. You ask the nurse, "What happened?" She tells you about the storm and the capsized cruise ship. She reports with sadness that hundreds are missing but then smiles as she informs you that you and your friend are some of the few survivors.

"But how? The last thing I remember was sinking beneath the waves. Everything went black. I was..."

"Dead?" she finishes the thought for you. "You were. But a man saw you and your friend go under. Even though it was very dangerous, he dove in and chased you down. He took hold of your lifeless bodies and pulled you to the surface. He dragged you to a nearby beach and performed CPR on you. He breathed into you and brought you back."

Your mind struggles to picture all that happened to you in your state of helplessness. You wonder why so many perished, but you were saved. Emotions of gratitude and unworthiness slosh around your mind and heart. It would take months, years, and even a lifetime to reconcile what had happened. But your reflections are interrupted as the door to your room bursts open. A small horde of reporters bombards the small space with cameras flashing and recorders held toward your face. There is a barrage of questions: "What happened? How did you survive? What was it like?"

You grimace at the assault on your eyes, but your friend suddenly commands all the attention by speaking.

"I'll tell you what happened. The storm was terrible! Those ships are designed to survive hurricanes, which should tell you just how bad this one was. Everyone on board had given in to fate. They surrendered to the storm and let it take them under. But not me! I like to keep a cool head. Even in chaos, I knew the only way out was to stay calm and trust in myself. Thankfully, I was on the swim team in high school and can hold my breath for a very long time. Even though our life vests were ripped away by the storm, I was able to save myself." Your friend continued their self-congratulating speech as reporters scribbled quotes and details.

You are shocked and perplexed by the fiction that pours from your friend's mouth. The reporters ask several questions and finally turn to you for more juicy details. As the cameras focus on you, the obligation of truth overwhelms you. With nothing to gain, you begin by saying, "I was helpless. I was dead. The waves took me under, and I sank to the bottom. But someone saved me! He saw me and rescued me. At great risk to himself, he pulled me to the shore and breathed life into me. There was nothing I could do for myself. I don't yet know who it was, but they deserve 100% of the credit."

9. Dual Tanks

The keys hung from his outstretched hand, his broad smile beaming with genuine excitement. I should have been excited or honored, but all I felt was concern.

"Are you sure about this?"

"Of course!" he said, the smile still frozen on his face. His eyes were not disingenuous. Still, I was skeptical.

I reached out and slowly took the keys. I had not yet driven off, so I wasn't past the point of no return. "It just seems like an unnecessary risk for a new hire. What's to keep me from driving it off a cliff or heading to Mexico?"

He laughed warmly, tilting his head back. Then he looked at me with just a touch of seriousness. "I think we can both agree that those possibilities are unlikely...and even silly. And I stand to gain much more from you taking care of it and using it for its intended purpose."

"And remind me again of what that is?"

"First of all, it's a resource. It allows you to travel, move things, shuttle people, and be helpful. Secondly, it's advertising. You can clearly see the company name on both doors and the tailgate. Every bit of exposure helps. Well, positive exposure, anyway. Take it—I bought it just for you."

I looked at the keys in my hand. Various scenarios of future successes and brutal failures tumbled through my imagination. He gave me a friendly pat on the shoulder and followed up with a squeeze. He smiled slightly, looked me in the eye, and said, "Now, go."

Heading away, I rolled down the windows and turned on the radio. *Man, this is nice.* I looked at the odometer slowly moving from 000,007 to 000,008 miles—so much life left in this vehicle. Even if it were abused and neglected, it could probably make it to 150,000. Twice that or more if I were to take care of it. This was nice. What a perk! I allowed myself to relax in the seat and enjoy the moment. The rest of the dash had the usual gauges: engine temperature, oil pressure, speedometer, and fuel gauge. Just to the right of the dash was a switch that allowed the operator to switch from one fuel tank to the other. I'd heard of bigger trucks having dual tanks and always wondered *why not just make the one tank twice the size?* Maybe there wasn't enough room for a tank that big. Maybe the fuel stays fresher with two. Maybe the extra tank was there in case you ran out of the first one.

To familiarize myself with the vehicle, I noticed the left tank was simply labeled "W," and the right was labeled "G." I raised an eyebrow at this peculiarity. The little light near the fuel gauge indicated that I was currently using the G tank.

My boss had explained the fuel situation and the dual tanks. The truck came with the G tank completely full. The W tank was virtually empty. He said that I would be reimbursed for any fuel I put into the W tank but that the G tank could be used freely as well. I had listened absentmindedly at the time, but now it seemed odd. More questions. Why not fill up both tanks? Or neither? Why not label the tanks "Left" and "Right" or "Mine" and "Yours"? I suddenly felt like I was abusing the boss's kindness. With a simple push of the switch, I changed to the "W" tank and pulled into a Mega-Mile station that was coming up on the right, and filled the tank.

Weeks went by, and I was putting the truck to good use. The cargo bed had its maiden scratches. It still looked brand new after taking it through the car wash every weekend. The odometer read 2,300, which equated to six fill-ups. I had developed the habit of filling my "W" tank when it got down to a quarter full. The "G" tank remained topped off and unused. *Perhaps there would be an emergency,* I thought, *or some stretch of highway with no stations.* Knowing it was there was quite comforting.

With time, I became more comfortable using the truck for personal errands. Yes, technically, I would be reimbursed for the fuel, so I tried not to abuse the privilege. But I was advertising everywhere I drove it. I tried to park around back when I went to the liquor store, and I really felt bad the one time I was on the shoulder getting a speeding ticket. Probably not the type of exposure the boss wanted.

So, it happened one day that I was towing my boat to the lake. It was completely gorgeous weather, and I was stoked. We were going to grill out, pull the kids on the kneeboard, and get some sun. My thoughts were already on the water when I noticed a minivan ahead on the shoulder. Its hazard lights were on, and it was sitting at that weird tilt that tells you one of the tires is completely flat. I slowed down out of courtesy and further diagnosed the situation as I passed by. There was a young lady in the driver's seat, head hung low and with an expression that was obviously one of frustration. In the rear of the van, I saw young kids standing who were apparently not contributing to her sense of peace (or lack thereof). *Poor thing,* I thought to myself. I started to accelerate away toward my family, my...obligations, and my much-deserved day at the lake when the truck started to sputter. My eyes scanned the dash for some indication of why the engine was suddenly bucking and coughing. Nothing was flashing, but I squinted at the fuel gauge. *That can't be.* My "W" tank was dropping fast, like there was a hole in the tank. It was passing the half-full mark and falling. I had just left the station not five miles earlier. *What gives? Stupid truck!* Without prompting, I was suddenly angry at my boss, angry at the company, mentally accusing them of giving me this piece of garbage to ride around in. This made no sense.

As I limped down the highway, further away from the stranded young lady, the truck seemed to protest even more. *I've got to get to the lake!* I was now brooding. What I wanted to do and what I should do were now embroiled in full-scale conflict. The truck was threatening to quit. My jaw was set in a frown as I looked at the tank switch. *Just press G. It will probably fix everything.* Why was I so reluctant? It was there to be used for this purpose. I was already taking advantage of my boss's benevolence. *Screw it.* I pressed the button. The fuel gauge needle suddenly moved upward to Full, and the engine began to purr. A smile crept over my countenance. Without delay, I braked hard and swung the truck in a wide arc, boat trailer and all. Now, pointed away from the lake, I accelerated hard. The engine roared as I sped toward my target, my mission. *Please still be there.* The speedometer needle crept past the legal limit, but surely this was justifiable. I watched the horizon and saw a speck on the opposite shoulder. Relief flooded my soul. Maybe I could make this right, for her and for myself.

I slowed as I neared. The young woman now had her forehead resting on the steering wheel. *Hopelessness.* The kids were entertaining themselves in the rear of the vehicle. Not wanting to scare her, I gave the horn a quick honk. As she looked up, somewhat startled, I waved and tried to appear friendly. She looked perplexed and concerned as I pulled behind her minivan and exited my vehicle. I continued to smile as I held both of my hands up around shoulder level. Hopefully, this was a universal sign that I meant no harm. I imagined how police officers must feel when they walk up to a vehicle. Her mascara was running from her tears, and the corners of her mouth were turned down.

"Hey! Can I help you out with your tire?" *Stay upbeat but sincere.*

It's like she hadn't considered that this situation could be fixed or made better. "Can you fix it?"

"Maybe. Do you have a spare?"

She looked around absently and then hopped out to open the back hatch. Sure enough, there was an old dusty spare, jack, and lug wrench.

"Alright! That's a good start."

She stood by and watched as I changed the tire. She didn't have the experience or the strength to help, as the lug nuts were almost stuck. I grunted and had to stand on the wrench for a few of them. But I suppose she would have felt rude sitting in the driver's seat. A few minutes later, the minivan was level again and ready to roll.

"Please stop at the next gas station to make sure it's got enough pressure," I suggested.

"Thank you so much. We are in the middle of moving, and we don't know anyone around..." her words became choked. Tears appeared in her eyes. "I'm sorry. It's just been a tough few months."

"And I'm sorry about that," I countered. There was a short pause before I said, "OK, Let's get these kids off the shoulder." I offered a smile.

"I don't have any way to pay you," she said, and she held empty palms toward me.

I thought it was interesting that we both had shown each other open hands as evidence of some deeper truth. It suddenly occurred to me that I could go further. I removed my wallet and pulled out two twenties and a ten.

"Here, you probably need gas money, and I'm sure the kids would like a snack."

She shook her head as more tears ran down her cheeks, but she did not reject my offer. I held the money closer and assured her, "It's OK; you'll be in a position to help someone someday."

She slowly took the money and then suddenly lunged toward me. My surprise was eased when she took me into a hug and offered the most earnest 'thank you' I'd ever heard.

As I turned the ignition on my truck, it obeyed without question. The engine was idling smoothly, and the tank still registered just above the Full line. *Interesting. You'd think it would have gone down a little with my hard acceleration.* As I got to highway speeds, I decided to try the W tank again. I pushed the switch and waited. Nothing happened—at least nothing that would involve a tow truck. But my eyes widened as I watched the fuel gauge needle rise all the way to Full.

This made no sense.

I was about forty-five minutes late arriving at the lake, but I felt wonderful. My mood must have been infectious because no one in my crew seemed upset or even to have noticed the delay. We had a great afternoon on the water, with abundant fun, and my conscience was clear.

The truck continued to serve me well. Like any vehicle, I began to discover its quirks. Every time it did something odd, I made a mental note to ask my boss about it. He'd laugh in his good-natured way and wave a hand in the air at my concern. "Ahh, you know trucks; they have their own personalities, just like we do." But I always felt that he knew more than he was letting on.

I was heading home from work several months later. Things had been going well on every front. My boss seemed thrilled with my performance. My wife appeared to be very proud of me. The truck had been a great resource for helping people. I'd learned that by being observant and surrendering to opportunities, I usually ended up coming out on top. *It's really weird.* I began to imagine scenarios where my truck and I would come sweeping in to save the day, hopefully for some damsel in distress. Then afterward, as people were singing my praises, I would gaze into the distance (possibly with my fists on my hips in a Superman pose) and say something like, "It's nothing that any noble man wouldn't do." *Glad no one else can see my imagination. How embarrassing!* Anyway, I was suddenly craving a cold beer. It wasn't illegal. It had less social stigma than smoking and was probably equal to overeating in terms of negative publicity. I continued to rationalize my decision as I parked the truck around the back of the liquor store.

A few minutes later, I was back on the highway, the cold six-pack peeking out of its paper bag. *Man, one of those would really hit the spot right now.* Technically, an open container was illegal, but I knew one beer would not put me anywhere near the legal limit. My mind was easily swayed, and my six-pack was suddenly a five-pack. The top was popped, and it went down so smoothly. *I deserve this.* After all, I was like a good Samaritan...for free! All the help I'd given had been on my time, mostly, and in my truck. I was basically on the same team as the police. They would understand.

She was walking on the shoulder away from me. As was my new habit, I slowed down to investigate. She was young and shapely. Her clothes were well-fitting and stylish. *Any man would have noticed.* I was concerned about her being out here, alone, so I slowed and rolled down the window.

"Need a lift?" I asked with my trademark smile and friendly tone. When she turned to look at me, I immediately noticed her eyes. She had on heavy makeup, but it was well done, dark, and mysterious. She gave me a cursory look and smiled coyly.

"Sure!" She opened the door and hopped inside. I decided not to say anything when she failed to buckle her seatbelt. For some reason, I felt that would be "uncool."

"Where to?" I asked, trying to sound casual.

"Just up the road a ways. I've got a friend that lives in the next town." She looked down at the six-pack, er, I mean five-pack, and then at my open beer. "May I?" she asked, cutting her eyes to my open beer in the console.

I was pretty sure she was over twenty-one, so I replied nonchalantly, "Sure. Be my guest." I was surprised when she took my beer and drank a long gulp. Seeing her lips where mine had been made my stomach quiver like a teenage boy's on a first date. The small red light flashing in my mind was now accompanied by a wailing alarm, but I rationalized *you aren't doing anything wrong. You're helping! Just be cool.*

Out of my peripheral vision, I caught glimpses of her holding my beer and fishing around in her jacket pocket for something. *Is she going to smoke? Do I want her to smoke in my truck?* I continued to drive when she suddenly gasped.

"Oh my gosh! I just realized I took your beer. Oops!" She put it back in the center cup holder. For some reason, the thought of drinking it after her lips had been on the can was so enticing. I could imagine traces of her lipstick. I took the can and took a big gulp, then another. My suddenly seventeen-year-old mind decided to chug the rest of it and then toss the can out of the window so that it rang the cargo bed. She watched me and smiled. *This feels dangerous. I like it.*

The events that followed were foggy. I woke up, slumped over in the seat, my head aching as if a mule had just kicked me. I blinked several times as I tried to make my eyes focus. My mouth was dry and sticky. As I sat up, I noticed I was parked on a dirt road in the middle of nowhere. There was nothing man-made anywhere in sight. I guessed I was still in my home state, but maybe not. I began to take inventory of myself and my truck. My leg was completely asleep from lying at a weird angle. The glove box was open, and its contents had been dumped on the floorboards. My pockets were turned inside out. I felt behind me for my wallet, but it was gone; so were my watch, wedding band, belt, and boots. Dread and humiliation filled my soul. *How could I have been so stupid! What am I going to tell my boss? What am I going to tell my wife? Where am I?*

I was in no shape to drive. The beer was missing, too, and I was terribly thirsty. Thankfully, the keys were still in the ignition. With no shoes, a bad case of dehydration, and the side effects of whatever it was she had drugged me with, walking out of here would be pretty much impossible. I turned the key, and the engine tried to crank. It spun and spun but barely sputtered. My eyes tried to read the gauges. Another pang of alarm. My "W" fuel gauge was way below the Empty mark. Apparently, she, or they, had driven me out into the desert until the truck ran out of gas. I slumped forward and let my forehead bang against the steering wheel. *What am I going to do?* It took a few minutes because my mind was working slowly, but a possible solution began to appear on the distant horizon of my thoughts. I focused until it drew near enough to recognize. *The other tank!* I quickly pushed the switch to "G" and hoped the needle would rise. My heart began to pound, the seconds passing like minutes. It started to move. It climbed upward, going past three-quarters and resting just above Full. *How has it never gone down at all?* I turned the key again, and the engine came to life after a few revolutions. *I'm saved!*

I drove the truck with a newfound respect. With nothing in my "W" tank, I was completely dependent on the boss's "G" tank. I was helpless without it. Yes, I felt shame and guilt. I also knew that there would be consequences. I could even get fired. Worse than that, my wife could hold this against me. Too much had happened for me to dare to try to cover this up with lies. I drove mile after mile back towards civilization, eyes glued to the fuel gauge. Increasing the distance from where I'd been and drawing closer to those to whom I would be accountable somehow provided me with comfort. I would fess up. I would take my punishment. I would reexamine my efforts, my motives, and who was providing my resources. I would learn from this. And the oddest thing of all, the needle never dropped below Full.

10. F-35

"**D**o I really have to wear this?" I asked as I stared disdainfully at the brown and white striped coveralls in my right hand. The large female, who I mentally referred to as "The Warden," just looked at me with equal aversion. It was oversized and made to be worn over clothing. We were minimal flight risk as far as criminals go. I slipped one leg in and then the other. I buttoned it up just above my waist and let the rest hang open. It would be a small but sustaining act of defiance.

As part of our community service, we would be picking up litter around the local air force base. It was some type of cooperative agreement between the court system and the federal government. In my mind, I couldn't imagine there being any trash on a military installation, but apparently, forced laborers like me are what allowed that image to hold true.

A quick bus ride through the gate, and the warden began to drop us off at designated areas. Each person was issued a roll of large garbage bags and a grabber. It was, in essence, a wooden pole with a mechanical claw on its end. Being given such an aid was both thoughtful and demoralizing. The type of people who used grabbers were either old or convicted.

The bus stopped, and I was deposited at the edge of the airfield. I was told to stay away from any pavement and to watch for planes. I wasn't sure if the warden was being serious or sarcastic. Another offender was already at work a few yards away. He was about twice my age but appeared healthy. He looked up and smiled at me.

Where are his coveralls? I wondered to myself. Maybe he had some chewing gum he'd be willing to share. Or maybe a cigarette? I walked over and stuck out my hand. "Hey. I'm Mike."

He shook my hand, smiled, and looked me in the eye. "Hi, Mike. I'm Chris."

He was also picking up trash, but I noticed his brand of trash bags was different from those I'd been given. And no grabber. That was strange. I felt a jab of jealousy that he was unencumbered and a puff of pride for the gadget I wielded. We humans are an odd bunch.

"So, where's your jumpsuit?" I asked. He looked confused by my question until he examined my stylish apparel.

"Oh. That type of jumpsuit. I didn't wear mine today. You probably didn't have a choice."

"No, I didn't," I said with as much sullenness as a twenty-one-year-old could muster. "The warden, I mean, Mrs. Jennings, was very clear that if we ditched the clothes or shirked our work, we'd be out here until we got it right." I know I'm officially an adult now, but the attitudes of a teenager are not very far in my wake.

Chris nodded understandingly and continued to scour the ground for debris. He stooped down and picked up a crushed soda can before depositing it into his bag. "Maybe we can walk the perimeter and stay about ten feet apart. We would cover twice the ground and still be able to talk," he offered.

"Sounds good to me." I was glad that he was friendly. The

tough-guy act that I'd been maintaining was taxing. We walked and worked as he asked about my life. His questions weren't intrusive, but he showed sincere interest and seemed to focus on anything positive that I mentioned. Like most people, I enjoy talking about myself, so I continued to bask in his interest. He didn't ask about my reasons for being here, but my need to tell him felt like bile building up in my throat. He was commenting on my desire to start trade school when I interrupted him.

"I shoplifted!" It came out loud, abrasive, and unsolicited. He stopped and looked at me.

"That's the reason you're doing community service. You shoplifted." It wasn't a question. He was restating to let me know he understood. There was an odd moment of silence as we stopped walking and stood there, staring at each other in the low grass. He looked away as if deciding how to proceed. Then he spoke. "It's obviously a big deal to you, so I guess it's not something you do often. What'd ya steal?"

Thieves steal things. I'm a thief. Not just a small-time shoplifter but a thief. The realization had a simultaneously stinging and soothing effect. Apparently, I needed to hear it from someone before I fully admitted it.

"It was stupid. I stole an MP3 player. I'm not even sure MP3s are still supported. But it was on a display right by the door. I was walking out and thought I could swipe it and put it in my jacket. It was a spur-of-the-moment decision. I had the money in my wallet to buy it, and I didn't even really want it. It just seemed easy. The next thing I knew, this big security guy was leading me back to the security room, where footage of me was being prepared for the police. They came and picked me up, and the rest is history."

Chris nodded as he digested the story. After a moment, he simply said, "I'm sorry." I wasn't sure what he was sorry for, but some sympathy felt good right about now.

"So, what about you? What'd ya do?"

He grinned and looked up at the sky as if recalling his offense. "I crashed a plane."

They stuck me out here with a terrorist? I looked away and then looked at the woods nearby. My mind selected an escape path just in case this got dangerous.

He could obviously discern my discomfort, so he expounded. "I had permission to fly it. I, uh, it was also stupid."

My silence goaded him to continue, albeit somewhat reluctantly. "I had just made Lieutenant Colonel, which is just above Major. Most of our squadron had recently completed being reclassed into the newer F-35 from the aging F-16. I guess being a fighter pilot always stokes your ego, but something in my mind was intentionally exceeding a deserved limit. With the new rank and access to the best plane in the Air Force, I began to feel invincible. One day, we were out on a training sortie. The mission parameters had us flying without external fuel tanks and running some flight patterns near the base. As we broke off one by one, I made one final pass by a mountaintop where I'd seen some hikers. For some reason, I wanted them to get a close look at Lieutenant Colonel Chris Hopkins and his new jet. As I buzzed them, it got the response I was looking for. They waved their arms and shot patriotic fists up in the air. I waved my wings and pulled a high-G turn before heading back to base. I didn't know it at the time, but my plane had a malfunction in the fuel transfer system." He paused and shook his head. "I was counting on those extra pounds of fuel to get me home, but I didn't make it."

I was riveted. Was this guy for real? I was expecting some story about bad checks or child support. But this? "What you do mean, 'you didn't make it'?"

He looked at me. "I ran out of fuel. I had to punch out. It was that or die. When I realized what was happening, part of me was tempted to go down with the ship. We'd trained for ejections, but you can't prepare yourself for what it's actually like. The canopy disappears, and a hurricane of wind slams your helmet back into the headrest. Then, your whole body is compressed into the seat as the rockets fire. Then, it's silence. The chute opens, and it's oddly peaceful. I was glad to be alive, but I watched as my jet coasted steeper and steeper and finally struck the side of a mountain. I was sure to point it away from anyone before we parted ways. Sitting there in the desert waiting on the rescue team gave me plenty of time to think."

Like many consolers, I tried to point out someone to blame. "But they sent you up in a broken plane. Man, you should sue those guys!"

"Had I not done my victory lap, that broken plane and I would have made it safely back to base. You can't expect the aircraft to be without issues. It's a man-made machine."

I gave him the moment of silence his story deserved. "So, what happened?"

"Out in the desert, I decided to come clean. I didn't hide anything during the investigation. I was knocked down to First Lieutenant and assigned to the heavies." My face must have registered confusion. "Heavies are military jargon for cargo planes."

I nodded as I absorbed this new knowledge. "So, they made you pick up trash to pay for the jet?"

He laughed more at himself than at my comment. "Oh, no. There won't be any paying for the jet. It would take generations of paychecks to cover that $70,000,000 debt."

"Seventy million dollars?" I said it with slow exaggeration and wide eyes. He nodded solemnly. This was way more serious than my shoplifting. "So why are you out here?"

"They showed me mercy. I can't ever pay it back, but I want to do anything and everything I can to show I appreciate it."

"So, you're picking up trash," I stated flatly.

"Today. Tomorrow, I think I'm teaching swimming lessons. Whatever they need."

So many questions in my mind. "So, when does it end?"

He paused to consider this. "I don't know. I'm in my mid-forties. They usually make you retire at sixty-two."

My mind was awash with the idea that he was so happily volunteering his time out here. He had not bashed the Air Force or called anyone a warden. What did that say of me, who totally deserved this and, truthfully, jail? It would tumble through my thoughts for the rest of the day. I felt honored to be picking up trash next to this man. I hoped that our paths would cross again. And to seal his place in my esteem, he suddenly turned to me and said, "Say, that's a nice grabber!"

11. In Control?

The pencil-shaped cone was quite pointless in this environment, pardon the pun. Even traveling at close to 535,000 kph, its shape might as well have been a box...or a parachute. In the vacuum of space, there was no air resistance, which meant there was virtually nothing to slow you down and little to keep you from speeding up. Thus, the Odyssey continued gaining velocity. It was all due to the recent advent of solar-assisted propulsion. A large solar reflector placed in a geosynchronous orbit transmitted limitless energy toward the rear of the ever-departing spacecraft.

The candidates for the mission were selected for their intelligence, temperance, youth, single status, and emotional stability. Paul had easily settled into the day-to-day rhythm aboard the ship. Most of the processes were automated and monitored by the ship's computer, but tasks were intentionally inserted into the astronauts' lives to maintain a sense of purpose and routine. He would wake up, exercise, eat breakfast, knock out the easy chores, and then procrastinate for the rest of the day as the computer nagged him with increasing intensity. It became a game for him to come up with new comebacks and sarcasm, which caused the 3rd Gen Hyper Computer to hiccup more than once. NASA was not a fan of this pastime.

Ted, on the other hand, had not yet mastered the art of shirking. Quite the opposite. He had developed a strange habit of sitting at the bridge station with his hands poised over the manual controls. Occasional beads of sweat would trickle down from his temple, in front of his ear, and then down his neck, where his carotid artery pulsed visibly.

Paul looked up from a magazine (which he'd read a dozen times through) and gave Ted a cursory glance just to make sure he wasn't doing anything too crazy, like opening an external hatch. *Poor guy,* Paul thought to himself. *They warned us about the possibility of going crazy.* Meanwhile, Ted scanned the infinite blackness punctuated by brilliant specks of white through the forward observation.

If earnest thought was given to the unfathomable speed they were traveling, it could cause paralyzing fear. After all, at that rate, they could travel around the earth thirteen times in one hour. Before it was replaced by the Global Deep Space Gateway, the International Space Station took ninety minutes to make just one orbit.

Paul had thought about this but reasoned that a collision at 70 mph with an asteroid would be just as deadly. Besides, the computer had calculated their odds of striking one to be the same as locating a single flea on the beach. Space was just that large and empty. Ted, on the other hand, had begun to fixate on that minuscule possibility.

Six years, eight months, fourteen days, twelve hours, two minutes, and fourteen seconds into their mission, Ted's worst fears were realized. The FLIR (or Forward-Looking Infrared Radar) began to flash a red warning light, which was accompanied by an intentionally annoying siren. Paul slowly lowered his copy of *War and Peace* and looked over its top at a bedraggled and very unhealthy Ted. Poor Ted's nerves were frayed, so the alarm caused him to topple backward off his crew chair. He scrambled back to his feet and leaned closer to the glass, hoping to catch a glimpse of the threat. At thirty-five years of age, Ted's temples were going gray, and his eyes had permanent dark circles underneath. Unlike the nicely bronzed Paul, he had been neglecting his daily visit to the ship's artificial sunlight generator.

"Paul! Get over here. I think I see something!" Ted's voice was shrill as he peered even closer through the windshield. His shaking hands hovered over the controls. He forced himself to rip his eyes away from the space before him, expecting to see Paul approaching at an urgent sprint. Horror filled his stomach as he saw that Paul had returned to his reading despite the flashing red light and blaring alarm.

"Paul! Ted shouted. "What are you doing? Are you crazy? We are about to hit something. I need your help!" Ted's voice was raspy and cracking. He returned his attention to the forward observation port, quickly monitoring the banks of lights and buttons on the console. He felt slightly relieved when he felt Paul slowly walk up beside him. *Good. He needs to be here helping me! He needs to be panicked. He needs to know how I feel.* Ted was horrified when, out of his peripheral vision, he saw Paul stretch his arms widely and yawn like a Cheshire cat.

He whipped his head towards his crewmate. "What is wrong with you? How can you be so obtuse? We are going to die!"

Paul raised his eyebrows only slightly at the fervent rebuke. He slowly lowered his hands and pressed a button labeled "cancel" on the console. The siren silenced, and the flashing light extinguished. Paul then scratched the right side of his stomach and rubbed it as he contemplated what would taste good as a snack right about now.

Ted was horrified. He stood there open-mouthed and stared in astonishment at his worthless crewmate. Silence ensued as the stare-down continued. Paul finally noticed that he was in the crosshairs of Ted's rage.

"Want some Doritos?" Paul asked warmly and sincerely.

Ted's mouth dropped open even further.

Paul couldn't help it—he chuckled. He immediately caught himself and apologized. "I'm sorry, Ted. I shouldn't laugh."

Ted lowered his chin because his mouth would not open any further. There was no way to increase his incredulity other than holding this pose.

Paul held his hands up and then slowly placed his left hand on Ted's shoulder. "Hey, bud. Can I show you something?"

Ted didn't know what to do or say. In his mind, the ship was about to burst into millions of splinters as an angry herd of asteroids sliced through the Odyssey's hull.

"I should have pointed this out to you years ago, but I thought you knew, and to be honest, I've been entertaining myself at your expense. I'm sorry." Paul's voice was earnest and kind.

"Show me what?" was all that Ted could say.

Paul nodded toward the console, indicating he wanted to man the controls for a moment. Ted slowly and reluctantly yielded his position. Paul then sat in the crew chair and reactivated the FLIR's alarm. The awful assault on their eyes and ears resumed.

Paul suddenly yelled, "We're all gonna die!" and frantically began swinging the controls in all directions. He pulled up, pushed down, and yanked the stick left and right. He then started frantically pushing buttons and flipping switches. Ted was bordering on shock and stood paralyzed by fear. "Eject! Eject! Eject!" Paul yelled as he mimed pulling handles near his ears and jumping up out of the chair. He jumped a foot in the air and landed firmly on both feet.

He turned towards Ted and smiled, hoping his performance had been entertaining.

Ted was not amused. "What...was...that?"

"I'm sorry, Ted. I really thought you knew. The controls don't work while we're in flight. They were disabled by the computer as soon as we departed from Global Deep Space Gateway. The buttons blink only to help us maintain confidence in this ship. It was one of those psychological safeguards they put into the mission. Didn't you read the manual?" Paul's expression was childlike in its innocence.

Ted was blinking as if he'd been stunned. "I was busy manning the helm."

Paul suddenly felt penitent toward his partner. "Ted, I am so sorry. I thought you knew and just couldn't help it. I feel horrible."

Both men knew that five years remained on this leg of their journey and an unknown amount of time for the next. Cold wars and silence were not an option in confined quarters. Paul decided right then to be more considerate of Ted's quirks for the rest of the flight, to help him find some levity and ignore the galaxy of "what ifs." Ted was obviously in serious need of some Vitamin D and a little Mexican comfort food.

Paul motioned toward the sunlight generator module and asked, "So, how about those Doritos?"

12. INSANE EMPLOYMENT

"I beg your pardon?" Apparently, I had not heard him correctly. "Could you please repeat that?"

The man on the other side of the desk continued to smile pleasantly. By appearances, he seemed of sound mind, but what he said was completely insane.

"Sure. If you come to work for me, I'll pay you your lifetime salary upfront. You won't have to worry about recessions, down markets, shortages, layoffs, etc. All you'll have to concentrate on is doing a good job—for me."

I sat there, bewildered, trying to process what he was proposing. It suddenly felt like I was in a time-share sales pitch where paradise is promised. Then, after you sign the contract, there's a truckload of fine-print obligations they failed to mention. I wanted to storm out of his office to show my indignation. I wasn't born yesterday.

But he was being kind—even friendly—and making an offer so ridiculous that I couldn't consider it seriously, even in the hypothetical.

"So, what you're saying is that you hire me, a stranger, then give me the millions of dollars I could make over decades of working for you before I even get a nametag."

"Wait a second." His face suddenly became serious. "I never said anything about a nametag."

We sat there looking at each other across the desk like gunslingers of the Wild West. Who would draw first?

"Haaaaa!" An enormous laugh escaped from a mouth smiling so widely that his eyes were all but invisible. "I'm sorry. Ohhh." He wiped a tear away. "You've got to admit, some well-timed humor can relieve a tense moment."

I was not laughing. I felt insulted. With a few years of experience in the rat race, I felt like I had a fairly good grasp of the concept of work and reward. It was always conditional. Pay followed the work if it met the standards. And excellent work should lead to extra compensation.

But this guy? I decided to play along. I don't know why, but I suddenly wanted to provoke him and wipe that silly grin off his face.

"OK. Well, this sounds great. I'm ready to sign up."

He nodded approvingly.

"But I've got a vacation planned for next month, so I'll be gone for two weeks."

"You definitely need to spend time with your family. We understand."

"And I'll need at least three breaks each day. If my blood sugar gets low, I could pass out—hypoglycemia." I was pretty sure that was the proper medical term.

"Of course. We understand that you have to eat."

He wasn't taking the bait. I decided to get more absurd. Really push the boundaries.

"And I'll need a company car and credit card for gas and expenses."

"Hmmm. To be honest, your initial duties may not require a company car. But if they ever do, one will certainly be provided. As a matter of fact, we have a company jet if the need arises." He casually lifted his hand and pointed toward a frame on the wall. He was in the photo standing in front of a gleaming white Learjet sitting outside an open hanger. Other planes were partially visible inside.

Checkmate. I couldn't rattle this guy. I decided to try directness. "Do you understand how crazy this all sounds to me? Look, you've been kind enough to give me your time, but this feels like a hidden camera show." I looked around the walls to see if there were any suspicious dark circles.

His expression became less jovial and more thoughtful. "I understand your doubts and how ludicrous this must sound. I've never claimed to be conventional. I make this offer to anyone interested in working for me. And I follow through with it. I offer the security up front that most people typically spend their whole lives fretting about. But, consider how it might affect an employee if he or she did not feel the constant pressure of performance evaluation. Imagine if you didn't have to worry about getting fired. What if you could make a mistake, even a big one, and not have to dread my wrath."

"Wrath? You don't seem like that kind of guy. Quite the opposite, actually."

"I don't like to be that person, but believe me, there are times that it is required and justified."

"Are you saying that I could really screw something up at great cost to your company, and you wouldn't do anything about it?"

"No. I'd definitely do something about it. But it would be for your good. Whatever that looked like, it would be to help you, improve you, and make you an even better employee."

I still could not get past how rational and reasonable he seemed. There was not even a hint of duplicity.

"So, what about the guy who takes the deal, grabs the money, and skips town? I'm sure that's happened."

His face became downcast. A sadness filled his eyes that seemed directly connected to his heart.

"Yes. That is one of the most tragic outcomes. It happens more than I'd like."

"So, what do you do about it? They owe you big time!"

"Yes. Their sense of indebtedness should make them loyal and dedicated employees. But instead, they misuse my kindness and go their own way. Sadly, when they leave my employment, the security they try to take with them tends to vanish, slip through their fingers. They are often too ashamed to come back and make amends. They end up worse off than when they began. It's not what I want."

"But you've got to have some limit to your capital. How can you dole out so many salaries and never run out?"

He smiled again and pointed to another frame behind him with his other hand. There he was, smiling (obviously) in front of a literal ocean of money. It stretched out into infinity. I was certain it was photoshopped, but it was oddly believable.

"So why? This all sounds too good to be true. Humans are not always very trustworthy. With your mindset, it seems like you're setting yourself up for disappointment."

"Yes. That's part of it." He leaned forward, and his gaze became intense. "But for those who get it, it is amazing. They serve me with complete joy. They trust me. They naturally do their best for me. You can't find a better employee than one who is personally devoted."

13. Maxed Out

Max had clean edges and well-defined numbers. His corners were smoothly rounded, and he glinted brightly when light was reflected off of his glittery face. His reverse side was smooth to the touch, the only exception being his faintly raised magnetic strip. He proudly displayed the family name, whose dimensional printing gave the illusion of being embossed across an alpine mountain scene. He was a handsome little card. Despite his youth and inexperience, he was identical in size to his older brother and his father.

His most enviable quality, however, was his balance (or lack thereof). Unlike most credit cards, he had never been swiped, charged, or accrued any debt. Not knowing any differently, he took his burdenless existence for granted. His brother had been spared from the abuse and misuse that most cards experience by working in the issuing bank.

Max remembered sitting around the campfire as scary stories were told. One in particular stuck out in his innocent mind. Apparently, a card was nestled safely in his leather nest, resting comfortably beside his friends. Through the layers of cowhide and denim, this card heard his handler complaining about "forgetting his keys" and "being locked out." The nest was extracted from its rear pocket, and he was chosen. But instead of the expected ATM slot or register, the guiding hand slowly moved him toward the edge of the door next to the handle. He was forced into the tight crevice and forcefully jammed into the dark space. Cold metal began to grind down his numbers, and he began to flex uncomfortably. That's when it happened—the card was bent.

Chipped edges could be lived with. Worn numbers were tolerated. But a crease? That meant no more swiping. You were basically useless. Yep. Once you were creased, there would be a brief phone call, and then you'd be suspended over the trash can. Your handler would then brandish a sharp pair of scissors and slowly transform you from one useful piece of plastic into tiny shards of trash. The storyteller had been successful in scaring the security codes right off of his captive audience. But he had to take it one step further by introducing them to the shredder.

But that was years ago, and Max was no longer a kid. He was becoming restless. His older brother seemed to flaunt the fact that he was already in circulation and even carried a paltry balance from time to time. When Max spoke to his father about it, Father would say, "Be patient. Your time will come. Enjoy this season of life. Let me carry the heavy loads." As a platinum card, Father's capacity had always been respected and admired.

One day, Max's brother passed by and casually mentioned that his own limit had been raised. Max didn't realize that this had been an automatic upgrade now that a year had passed with no indiscretions. The gloating had its desired effect. Max stormed up to his father and said, "I want to be activated now!" He had never spoken to his father in that tone, but he meant business. No more would he sit in his brother's shadow. No. He would be put into circulation and see the world. He was just as capable as any card (or so he thought). Max had the strip, the numbers, and a far-off expiration date. His father's normally rectangular posture seemed to wilt at the edges as he asked, "Are you sure this is what you want?"

Anger is hard to control when you're young. "Yes!" declared Max, "I want it, and I don't care how. Transfer your balance, get bent, or find a shredder. I don't care."

His father silently nodded his assent, and the transaction was complete. Max sullenly turned away and was soon secured in a Naugahyde nest. It was time to see the world.

His handler was just as young and naïve as Max was. Oh, the fun that they had together. Burger, fries, and milkshake? No problem. Swipe. New shoes for basketball? Sure! Swipe. Two movie tickets? "It's my treat." Swipe. On and on it went. Max felt drunk with purchasing power. It was effortless. Just a quick, painless swipe, and you could have anything you wanted. There were rock concerts, tanks of gas, a cool leather jacket, and an unsuccessful trip to the liquor store. How had his father deprived him of this freedom for so long?

Then, one day, Max heard a word that was new to him. He and his handler were in a convenience store. The counter was littered with beef jerky sticks, a large slushy, and a bag of powdered donuts. Max was removed from the wallet and swiped, as he had been so many times before. But the keypad suddenly made a strange beeping noise. The clerk swiped Max again and frowned. The handler looked perplexed as Max learned this new word. "Denied."

As they left the store empty-handed, Max's handler tapped him in his empty palm as if trying to decide what to do next. The sensation of uncertainty and nausea formed in what would have been his stomach. There was a trash can nearby on the sidewalk, and for a moment, Max looked around in a panic for the sudden appearance of scissors. But the handler shoved him back into the cheap leather-like lair as he complained about his "cheapskate parents."

The next few weeks were a miserable blur of neglect and mistreatment. Max stayed in the wallet for days with no fresh air or sunshine. One chilly morning, he was withdrawn and used to scrape frost from a windshield. His upper edge sliced through the ice and over the carcasses of dead bugs. It was demoralizing. Days later, he was again extracted and slid along the underside of his handler's shoe. Someone's chewed gum, speckled with road grime, was now caked in the crevices of his once-pristine numbers. His sharp edges were now pocked with nicks. How had this happened?

Rock bottom would happen the next day around lunchtime. Max's handler was loitering near an outdoor café. As a nearby couple paid their bill and left the restaurant, the young man quickly swooped up the lady's half-eaten burger and a handful of the man's uneaten fries. He ate the leftovers as he briskly walked away down the urban sidewalk. Apparently, an onion had become lodged in the handler's upper teeth. Like a toothbrush demoted to bathroom cleaning duty, Max was pulled from the wallet, and his now deformed corner was wedged into his handler's mouth. The odor was atrocious. Max blanched at the mustard-laced saliva that now coated his once-smooth surfaces.

If there was a redeeming aspect to brokenness, it was his newfound contrition. Gone completely was the jealousy of his brother. Instead of resenting his father's attempts to protect him, he longed to be clean and financially solvent. *How do I get back there?* He wondered to himself. *How could I ever clear this astronomical balance?* The faint possibility of restoration was the only spark of light in this hopeless night of darkness.

The "cheapskate parents" finally located their wayward child with the nice sneakers and cool leather jacket. He was allowed to keep those mementos, but Max was confiscated. He was placed in an envelope and delivered to a building that somehow felt familiar even though veiled by his paper enclosure. The next day, the seal was broken, and he was removed. The bank! Somehow, he was back at home. He saw his dad running toward the nearest keypad. Suddenly, his balance had been upgraded to the seemingly limitless volume of his father's. Max's father drew near and began to repair the tattered edges and worn numbers. Max wanted to fabricate an excuse, but all that came out was a choked apology. "I'm so sorry, I was..." But his father would not let him finish. "It doesn't matter. You're back, and you're safe." The mending and tending continued. Max relented and surrendered to the care.

Everything was right with the world again. Max's appearance was similar to his former state, with only small visible reminders of his time in circulation. That evening, the family celebrated. Everyone seemed so pleased that Max was back except for his older brother. Their father left the party to check on him.

"Hey, big guy," Father said, "Don't you want to join us? We're about to break out some bonus miles."

His firstborn turned away sullenly. "Bonus miles? You're giving Max bonus miles? After the way he disgraced our family name? And you? I have been so faithful in picking up lunch, paying for dry cleaning, and buying cleaning supplies. He hits his limit on junk, and you act like it's no big deal." The air was heavy with animosity. "I hate him."

When he was younger, such language would not have been tolerated. But with a fantastic amount of paternal patience, his father said, "You've always been the responsible one, and one day, you too will be a platinum. But rising above unfairness is the only path to that destiny."

14. OPPOSING TWINS

"All rise." the bailiff commanded in a nasal, authoritative voice. There was the shuffling of shoes and the squeaking of pews as everyone stood to their feet. An African-American woman wearing a floor-length black robe entered from an ornate wooden door at the front of the room. She made her way to the center podium, also known as "the bench." She gave little attention to the people standing in recognition of her position until she sat in a high-backed leather chair. After scooting up to her workspace, she looked up. She performed a cursory inspection of the room and its occupants before blandly stating, "Be seated." Again, there was the muted clamor of people getting comfortable.

She opened a file and stated, "We are here today on the case of State vs. Johnson. Is the prosecution ready?"

A suit-clad middle-aged man stood. His dark hair was tinged with gray near the temples. He responded confidently, "Yes, your honor."

"And the defense. Is your client present?"

A surprisingly young woman wearing a smart business-style blouse and skirt stood respectfully. She looked at an equally young woman to her left before responding, "Yes, your honor. We are here."

The judge nodded as both the man and woman took their seats. The air was thick with the gravity of what was about to occur. There would be official accusations with consequences that could separate families and suspend constitutional freedoms. There was no quarter for levity.

"Call your first witness," the judge said flatly as she picked up a pen and held it over a yellow legal pad.

The dapper prosecutor stood again. "Your honor, the state calls Marcy Dunnegan."

A young woman with a pensive demeanor was led into the room by the bailiff. He directed her to a wooden enclosure called the "witness stand."

Before sitting down, the judge directed her to "raise your right hand." The woman complied sharply. "Do you swear to tell the truth, the whole truth and nothing but the truth, so help you God?"

"Yes, I do," the woman said while nodding in the affirmative.

"Be seated."

The prosecutor approached with a broad but practiced smile. "Could you state your full name for the court, please?"

The woman leaned forward and spoke into a small microphone mounted on the front rail. "Marcy Denise Dunnegan."

"And in the course of your daily duties, have you come to know the defendant, Mrs. Teressa Johnson?"

"Yes, I know her."

"Could you point to her, please?"

The lady on the stand pointed to the woman sitting at the defense table on the left side of the courtroom. The target of that gesture seemed present and very much at ease. It was almost peculiar, considering what she was potentially facing.

"And how do you know Mrs. Johnson?"

Again, she leaned forward. "She's my neighbor. She lives directly across the street from me."

"And how long have you been neighbors?"

"A little over a year."

"Can you please tell the court about the first time you saw Mrs. Johnson?"

"It was last spring, and the house across the street had been for sale. We were wondering who our new neighbors were going to be. One day, the for-sale sign was missing, and a moving truck was in the driveway. Naturally, I looked outside to see who was moving in. Her husband walked around to the passenger side, opened her door, and helped her out."

"And why did she need help?"

"She was very pregnant. I took one look at her and said to my husband, 'That woman has got to be expecting twins.' That's when he said..."

"Hearsay, your honor!" It was the studious-looking woman beside the defendant. She had popped to her feet before making her objection.

The judge nodded to the defense and then addressed the witness. "You are not allowed to testify to what other people said. You can only relate your own statements and thoughts."

The slightly shaken witness nodded that she understood and concluded, "She was unusually large in her belly."

The prosecutor chuckled at the comment to ease the tension and steady the witness. "So, was she, in fact, pregnant?"

"Yes. Turns out I was right. The couple came back from the hospital a week later and hauled in two car seats. They both had blue blankets, so I assumed they were boys."

"Did you see these children again?"

"Yes, I did. Often. The babies would spend a lot of time

outside, sitting on a blanket in their front yard. The parents didn't hide anything."

The prosecutor, who had been methodically pacing back and forth as he listened, raised an eyebrow. He turned and asked, "Why would you use the phrase 'hide anything'? Did you observe anything that would cause suspicion or concern?"

The witness looked down like a child being forced by their parents to tattle on themselves. "Well, we started to notice some differences."

"Differences?"

"More like favoritism. It wasn't hard to see that the parents doted on one of the babies and pretty much ignored the other."

There were faint gasps and murmurs in the audience.

"Objection, your honor!" It was the lady on the left of the defendant again. "The witness has not been recognized as a subject matter expert on child welfare."

The judge dully stated, "Sustained. Does the state have evidence of the witness's qualifications to make such assertions?"

The prosecutor asked the witness, "Mrs. Dunnegan, do you have children?"

She leaned forward and answered, "Yes."

"Specifically, do you have twins?"

"Yes, two boys, five years old."

"Do you believe that your experience as a mother equips you to make basic observations and come to reasonable conclusions in a similar manner to any sensible person?"

"Yes, I believe so."

The judge ruled without looking up from her doodling. "Continue."

"What do you mean by favoritism?"

For the first time, the witness redirected her attention to the defendant. It was subtle, but her visage took on a slightly hostile expression.

"She clearly spends most of her time with the smaller boy. The other boy is noticeably chubby. But the little one, she holds him almost constantly. She plays with him, talks to him, makes funny faces, and does everything you'd expect a mother to do."

"But what about the...chubby baby? How would you describe her interaction with him?"

"It's like she doesn't know him. It's like he's a stranger or something. I would expect anybody who saw a poor, helpless baby just lying there all alone would go over and scoop him up or something. But she ignores him."

The defendant sat there with a neutral countenance. If these words stung, she didn't show it.

"And observing these behaviors concerned you enough to call the authorities?"

"Well, I called my pediatrician first. He's the one that said I should call the authorities."

"Objection, your honor! Hearsay!"

The witness corrected her testimony. "Sorry. I called my pediatrician, and then I called the police."

The judge blinked her eyes but remained silent.

The prosecutor seemed very pleased and content. "We pass the witness."

He sat as the well-dressed woman stood and exchanged places with him.

"Mrs. Dunnegan. Do you monitor the parenting styles of all your neighbors or just my client's?"

The witness was suddenly defensive. "Well, the Johnsons live directly across the street. I can't help but notice what they do. They're out there for the whole world to see."

"I see. Do you compare the quality of the care Mrs. Johnson provides with your own? Are you setting the standards for what good parenting is?"

The witness shifted uneasily in the wooden chair. "Well,

nobody's perfect, but at least I don't neglect my kids!" Nerves had been touched.

"Have you ever disciplined one of your children for misbehaving?"

"Well, sure. But any good parent disciplines their child."

"And if someone saw you in that moment, would you have the appearance of a loving mother?"

Mrs. Dunnegan looked around the courtroom for help. She stammered, "I...they...they would need to know the whole story if they just saw me in that moment."

"No further questions, your honor."

The witness tried to continue. "It's just that..."

"Nothing further, Mrs. Dunnegan," the judge said firmly. "You can step down." Now somewhat shaken, the witness stepped down from the stand, feeling like she'd been on trial.

"The state calls Dr. Douglas Whitfield." It was the prosecutor again.

A dignified man close to sixty years of age with round spectacles and a ring of hair surrounding a shiny dome was led to the stand. He faced the judge and lifted his right hand expectantly before being sworn in. Then he sat down with an air that implied, "I'm doing everyone a favor by gracing them with my presence."

The prosecutor began. "Would you please state your name?"

With a coolness, he paused briefly for effect before saying, "Doctor Douglas Seymour Whitfield." If people's names are their favorite words in the English language, he certainly enjoyed his.

"And would you tell the court about your profession and field experience?"

"Certainly. I am the senior pediatrician at the Jamestown Medical Plaza and have been licensed to practice medicine for over thirty years. I completed a fellowship in adolescent psychology at the University of Devlin. I served on the board of the Winston Childhood Development Center. In 2018, I received the award for..."

"Thank you, doctor." The prosecutor mercifully spared everyone from an endless list of accolades. "And in the course of your business, have you had interaction with Mrs. Marcy Dunnegan, the previous witness?"

"Yes. Her sons have been under my care since their birth."

"And would you say, based on your medical expertise, that Mrs. Dunnegan appears to be of sound mind and capable of making reasonable observations?"

"Mrs. Dunnegan presents herself as an intelligent, capable, and well-informed individual. I've seen no reason to question these attributes."

"So, if Mrs. Dunnegan had concerns about another child, it would be reasonable to give them your consideration?"

"Of course. I would be derelict in my duties to ignore such concerns."

"Have you responded to any concerns Mrs. Dunnegan may have discussed with you?"

The doctor was smart enough to avoid answering in a way that would be considered hearsay. "I advised Mrs. Dunnegan to call the police based on my assessment of the situation."

"And what situation are you referring to?"

"The circumstances concerning her neighbor, I believe, Mrs. Johnson." He nodded and pointed to the lady seated at the table on the left. His tone was suddenly grave.

"Did you at any time call family services or the police?"

"No. I did not feel it was my place since I had no personal knowledge of that family." His last two words were tinged with disdain.

"All right. I want to ask you some general questions about

child welfare. Have you ever seen a case of failure to thrive stemming from a lack of attention or affection?"

"Objection, your honor! Leading the witness." The defense attorney almost shouted as she popped up out of her seat.

The judge unemotionally addressed the prosecutor. "Sustained. Prosecutor, rephrase your question."

"Yes, your honor." He turned back toward the witness. "Are you familiar with the condition referred to as failure to thrive?"

"Yes, of course."

"And what would be the common causes of this condition, in your experience?"

"It's not often seen in the United States, but in third-world and communist orphanages, children have suffered and died directly from a lack of attention and/or physical affection."

"So, if I understand correctly, depriving a child of attention or physical affection would constitute neglect or mistreatment?"

"Yes, it would."

"I pass the witness, your honor." The prosecutor sat down, hoping that the finality of the last statement would leave an impression on the jury.

The defense attorney stood up and began. "Mr. Whitfield, I..."

"That's Doctor Whitfield," he quickly corrected.

She feigned embarrassment and said, "Forgive me." And with exaggerated emphasis, continued. "DOCTOR Whitfield. Do you have experience or knowledge relating to twins?"

With a great deal of smugness, he answered, "Yes, relating to both fraternal and identical. In 2016, I attended...."

"Thank you, doctor," she said, cutting him off. "Does the similarity of appearance or genetics also relegate twins to having similar personalities, tastes or preferences?"

"Not necessarily. Some traits are intrinsic, whereas others

are developed through experience and environmental influence."

"So, it's fair to say that if a mother had twins, her interactions would need to be specific to that child's personality and associated needs?"

He shifted uncomfortably in his chair for the first time. Even a casual observer could detect some bias in his testimony. "Well, the nuances of personalities open endless variables, especially in developing adolescents. It would require a study..."

She interrupted. "Just a simple yes or no will suffice."

The doctor visibly blanched at being reprimanded. "Young lady, I will not be disrespected by someone subordinate to me in their education and professional experience."

She replied coolly, "So, my interactions with you should be fashioned to appease your need for recognition?"

If he was unnerved before, livid was now a more accurate description. His head was turning red as he twisted it on his neck like something was about to burst out. He shut his eyes and tried to recenter himself. "I'm just saying that..."

"No further questions for this witness, your honor." With that, she daintily sat down and shuffled through some mostly blank sheets of paper. The doctor looked helpless and humiliated. After another awkward moment, the bailiff led him off the stand, leaving a trail of ignominy.

After a moment, the prosecutor stood and announced, "We have no further witnesses at this time, your honor." He and anyone else familiar with criminal trials wondered if the defense would be foolish enough to call the defendant to the stand. According to the Constitution, citizens were not required to testify against themselves. By opening a line of questions, the defendant would also be subject to cross-examination by the prosecution. It would be a slaughter that he would secretly relish.

The defense attorney stood. "Your honor, we call Mrs. Teressa Johnson." Murmurs and whispers could be heard throughout the room. The prosecutor's lips pulled back into a tight, thin smile.

If the defendant was worried, her body language did not show it. She stood before the judge, raised her hand, and was sworn in like the others before her. The judge added, "You understand that the slightest alteration or avoidance of the truth will constitute perjury?" It was hoped that the judge would be completely objective in this case, but no human is exempt from partiality.

"Yes, your honor." The young lady sat in the seat and scanned the faces of the jurors. Some avoided her eyes, fearing they would soon be required to determine her sentence.

The defense attorney began, "Could you state your name for the court?"

"Teressa Marie Johnson."

"And could you state your occupation?"

"Housewife, mom, cook, diaper changer, maid." Her answer did little to relieve the tension in the room.

The defense attorney played along. "And how long have you served in these positions?"

"I've been married for three years and became a mom last April."

"Do you have any frame of reference for assessing the health or normalcy of your relationships with your spouse or children?"

"Objection, your honor!" It was the prosecutor. "Proper foundation has not been laid for this witness."

"Overruled." The judge flatly replied. "The court takes judicial notice of her experience as a wife and mother."

The prosecutor sat down. The disruption had been his surreptitious goal.

"Please continue, Mrs. Johnson."

"Well, I was a child. I had parents. I've seen countless other children and parents. So, I understand what a (she made air quotes with her fingers) normal family is. "

"And has your personal experience coincided with the 'normal experience' you were expecting?"

"No. It has not."

Everyone wondered where this was heading.

"Could you please share with the court what has been abnormal about your experience?"

She took a deep breath and turned to address the jury. "I'm not sure what I was expecting. You see advertisements and television shows where the mother gently holds and nurtures her babies. The children, in return, appear so comfortable and content. We began to notice within days of leaving the hospital that our two boys had drastic differences in their physical and emotional needs."

"Could you expound on these needs for the court?"

"So, Mike is totally infatuated with the physical. He wants to eat, have his diaper changed, and suck on his bottle. He wants the softest pajamas, the softest blankets, and the perfect temperature. He demands particular toys and refuses to share them with his brother. He fusses and cries the instant any of these conditions are less than optimal."

The defense attorney smiled. "This doesn't sound that unusual."

"It might not be until you compare him with Mark. Mark is just the opposite. He only wants to be near me. He loves being held close. He loves the sound of my voice. He stares fondly into my eyes. He gives me his attention when I call his name. Spending time with me and getting to know me is the most important thing in his life. I wasn't expecting this. Or maybe I was expecting Mike's and Mark's behaviors to be present in both of my boys. Just not extreme sides of both natures."

"What do you mean by both natures?"

She answered as if it should be obvious. "The physical and spiritual. Mike only wants what I can tangibly give him. He cares only about his physical needs and comfort. Mark, on the other hand, couldn't care less about those things. Believe me, I've tried to offer the opposite, but the results have been consistent. Mark wants and needs something that can't be grasped or measured. As a mother, I see no other choice but to meet their specific needs."

You could see the wheels of the jurors' minds turning.

"So, have your sons been given a clean bill of health from their pediatrician?"

"Yes. I have the paperwork from all of their checkups."

"And could you force Mike to be held and Mark to be fed?"

"I suppose I could, but that sounds like abuse."

"No further questions of this witness, your honor."

15. Painful Portal

In the days before nuclear fusion, this story would have never been possible. But on September 7th, the world suddenly changed. It had changed twice before, in 1760 and again in 1870, with the first and second industrial revolutions. However, those now seemed like mild tremors in terms of the magnitude of their impact. The Earth is now shaking with the implications of this new technology. The possibilities were endless. For the first time in human existence, people were using the term Utopia collectively and professionally. It really seemed like it could happen.

To recap, fusion has occurred throughout our universe since its inception. Two atomic nuclei with a comparatively lighter mass would be compelled to crash into each other. However, the force required would have to exceed their repulsive magnetic strengths, both having a positive charge. Instigating this nuclear canoodling, of course, requires copious amounts of heat, pressure, and confinement. When all conditions are perfect, the colliding nuclei merge to become a singular nucleus. The sum of this new mass would be less than the total of their separate masses, which means that we now have some leftovers. So, we bag 'em and enjoy them the next day as lunch or, in technical terms, store or harvest their energy.

Professor Douglas Higland was working late at the Bear's Ears Atomic Research Facility. The barren yet beautiful tract of land in southern Utah had long been the center of debate and controversy regarding its usage. However, the prospect of endless, clean energy had lightened everyone's mood (even in Congress!). Everyone seemed more willing to work together since an almost limitless prosperity was suddenly on the table. And since unsightly pipelines and drilling towers were rapidly becoming obsolete, no one really minded the construction of the 1.2-billion-dollar underground research facility. All that could be seen was a two-lane access road disappearing into a nondescript opening at the bottom of a sandstone butte.

However, the wow factor was evident to anyone allowed clearance to enter this subterranean lair. Foreign dignitaries and scientists would inevitably visit this premier laboratory, so no expense was spared. From the fully automated decontamination chamber to the holographic personal assistants, it seemed like a science fiction movie had been brought into reality.

The good professor viewed his duties as solemn. He felt he was actually writing history and could imagine his grandchildren reading about his work in their history books. He knew he had the intellect, wisdom, discipline, and determination to efficiently explore and apply this new technology. His assistant professor, lamentably, did not. Professor Gabe Gadget was a perplexing mystery to him. They had always had a courteous and somewhat professional relationship, but his observations of his supposed peer always tickled his suspicions. After watching Gadget accidentally set his lab coat on fire twice in one week, Higland wondered to himself, does he actually have his bachelor's degree...or even a GED? But in Gadget's defense, his slipshod behavior went hand in hand with unorthodox creativity, which led to some amazing breakthroughs. Nevertheless, Higland still theorized that Gadget's father must be a senator. How else could he have landed such a prestigious position?

Their latest experiment used twin focused-fusion rays to study the effects on the Earth's gravitational pull. They knew light and radio waves could be distorted using this process, but what about gravity? Two vertical laser transceivers were set like goalposts, their beams bouncing back and forth until a solid energy grid appeared. As he gazed into the rectangle of undulating blue static, Higland resisted its hypnotic lure. The waves of rippling energy, which syncopated with the ebbs and flows of its humming static, could quickly lull you into a trance. He closed his eyes and shook his head to focus on the Maston Gauge. It flickered, which was an excellent sign because gravity was supposed to be as constant as our planet's mass. He looked back at the surging panel suspended in open space not thirty feet away.

As his eyes fixed on some point beyond the veil of energy, Higland began to imagine the possibilities of hover cars and warp-drive spacecraft. Unbeknownst to him, Gadget had left the lab in a hurry just two hours earlier. When Gadget grabbed his jacket from the nearby coatrack, it had tilted several degrees and had come to rest against the corner of his desk. Apparently, the nearby fluctuations of gravity had caused it to slide along the edge of the desk, where it completed its fall by striking the rolling desk chair. The chair began to roll directly toward the backside of poor, unsuspecting Professor Higland.

He had unconsciously moved closer to the energy grid panel and was now squatting, fully transfixed on the living illusion that slithered now less than twenty feet away. The power intensified as he used his thumb to spin the wheel on the controller. His head snapped backward as the impact with the rolling chair occurred. The rest of his body, however, splayed forward clumsily. He tried to outrun his fall, but his bent legs made the movement even more spastic. He realized he was stumbling directly toward the experiment. His mind's automated preservation processes told his legs that it was preferable to fall face first instead of continuing on his currently terminal trajectory. He landed hard on his hands, chest, and face. To his horror, he was still sliding toward the blue rectangle, its static now felt in his hair and clothing. Adrenaline surged through his arms as he flung them out, wildly grasping for any hold. Nothing was within arm's reach, so he spun around and tried to palm the smooth, polished concrete floor. His hands made a squeegee sound as they unsuccessfully fought for purchase. He looked toward his feet, which were now dangerously close to the wall of blue lightning. The sensation initially felt like the tingling when your foot goes to sleep, but as the panel sucked him closer, it became like needles and then like electric knives.

The controller lay helpless on the floor and seemed to be moving further away. The searing pain moved up his legs toward his torso. It took his breath away but mercilessly left him fully conscious. As it moved into his chest and shoulders, he tried to scream but had no air in his lungs. The agony of asphyxiation was pleasant compared to the torture which infiltrated every cell of his being. It was a nightmare coming true. Every millisecond seemed like a minute as he was slowly sucked into the portal. He now wished for death as even a moment more seemed unbearable. In one final onslaught, blue light scorched his eyes as his world went black.

Or maybe blue. Black, blue, pink, purple. It didn't matter. As a matter of fact, nothing mattered. Higland's thoughts turned back to gravity and how it had been the source of so much discomfort back on Earth. Constantly adjusting in your seat, buying thick insoles for your shoes, falling to the hard, unforgiving ground when you're learning how to walk. But now, without any...it was blissful weightlessness. No pressure anywhere. And his eyes. We know that, to the eyes, all perceived objects are merely reflected light waves that land on the retina, interpreted by the occipital lobe. Using binary vision, they decipher distance, shape, texture, and dozens of other attributes to help identify the item. But that was no longer necessary. Nothing to see. Nothing to strain the eyes. He had acute awareness...but did he have eyes?

And what of stress? It's one of those things that you don't register until it's gone. But this was more than the absence of stress. It was the joy, peace, and security that resided on the other end of the spectrum. Had he ever been so unconcerned in his whole life? Thinking back to the mindfulness exercises he'd learned at a work retreat, he completed an inventory of his senses. It was...how could he describe it...the best of life amplified and permanent. He had no fear of it ending. It felt as though the intensity of this blissful state could expand pleasantly into infinity.

Time no longer existed. In the furthest corner of his memory, he recalled time on Earth being like a rope that you pulled yourself along hand over hand. This was more like floating and swimming in any temporal direction you chose. Experimenting with these movements only added to the bliss.

His accomplishments in life, titles, and awards all seemed less than trivial. A new wave of joy swept through him as he saw them disappearing into a cosmic trash can. Since words like frustration and challenge were now foreign to him, he considered the ardor of life to be worth this recompense regardless of its cost. That's when the pain returned.

It was just as agonizing as before but in reverse order and over very quickly. Highland lay on his back in the lab, his head rolling loosely on his neck. As his eyes fluttered and he tried to focus on the overhead lights, a face began to come into view. Gadget. A profound sense of loss swept through him. It was worse than being woken by ice water. It was worse than the death of a loved one. It was worse than being born into a cold, cruel world. He was back. It was over. And now he was alone with Gadget.

"Man, I thought you were toast!" Gadget exclaimed, sounding very much like a surfer. "I got all the way home and realized that I left my wallet on the desk. I came around the corner, and all I could see was the top of your head just inside the test stand. I probably should have killed the power, but all I could think of was pulling you out! Man, that hurt!" Gadget was massaging his own hands.

Higland rolled to his side, regaining normalcy by the second. But the infinite sorrow remained.

"One time in Australia, I got stung by a Portuguese Man of War." Gadget was almost rambling. "Man, that was nothing compared to the pain I just felt in my hands. You'd better be glad I like you, or I would have just let you keep cooking. You'd probably be well done by now!" He laughed like a ninth-grader in a locker room.

Higland slowly stood and made his way to his chair. He sat down, looking at the area that had been the blue portal. The memory of what had been came flooding back, and he began to weep. He cupped his hands over his eyes and sobbed. This life now seemed wretched.

"Dude! It's OK. You're back! You gotta be more careful, bro. Are you, like, just super happy to be alive and stuff?" Gadget's condolences were like fingernails on a chalkboard. But Higland was a scientist. His mind shifted gears, and he decided that feigning normality would be the quickest way for Gadget to leave.

Higland smiled, forced a chuckle, and stuck his hand out to shake Gadget's. "You really saved my neck. Thank you. And you're right. No more experimenting alone. I'll make sure you're here from now on so that neither of us misses anything good." It was terrible acting, almost like an episode of The Brady Bunch, but it seemed to be working. Gadget fished his wallet out of his top desk drawer and turned to leave.

"Later, dude! See ya' Monday." Footsteps faded. "Glad you're not toast!"

After hearing the door close, he fell to the floor. His analytical mind raced to process what had just happened. He'd always been pragmatic about existence...but what if there was more? Scientifically speaking, there are always unknowns. Existential evidence is superior in the courtroom of one's own mind. He also reflected on the pain that preceded the portal. It was beyond horrifying. Given his choice of demises, he would gladly take the guillotine, a steamroller accident, or a shark attack over what he had endured. However, their gruesome details were inconsequential if they all led to the same idyllic state. It posed the question, what would man endure to experience paradise? But his newfound awareness of the other side had somehow invalidated his fear. He would actually welcome the blue portal to reach what lay beyond.

16. Playground Dad

I was watching him watch someone. He sat on a park bench, holding a newspaper out in front of him as if he were reading. However, I noticed that this was just a ruse because his eyes were actually monitoring two small boys on a playground about fifty feet away. The two boys, probably around six or seven years of age, were playing in the dirt and making small talk the way that young boys do. Both of them had their attention focused on some toy cars that were plowing their way around the bits of gravel and sand.

After a while, the boys redirected their interest to an unusually tall slide that was just a few feet away. Judging from its height, the slide was probably constructed before threats of liability and lawsuits were commonplace. They slid their cars up the slide from the bottom and let them roll and spin back to their position. Suddenly, one boy pointed toward the ladder, and they both dropped their cars to head that way.

One boy was crawling up the rungs when the other began to follow. Suddenly, the man on the bench cleared his throat and rattled the paper as he turned a page. The boy at the bottom looked toward the bench and slowly aborted his ascent. The other boy commented from the top and made "BAWK BAWK" sounds of a chicken before sliding down. His hands were raised, and he made a point of shrieking his pleasure.

The two boys continued to explore the playground. All the while, the man sat on the bench with the two of them just in view over the paper's edge.

A few minutes later, a young voice of protest could be heard. It was answered by another. The paper lowered ever so slightly. The boy who had gone down the slide had both cars in his hand, and the other was trying to retrieve one of them. The voices escalated, and soon, push came to shove. It was a clumsy fight where lack of combat experience and exaggerated facial expressions stripped it of seriousness. Yet, no one wanted any actual pain or injury for the boys.

I watched the man as he monitored but chose not to intervene. It seemed like bad parenting to me. To allow this was to encourage it. Was he trying to raise two brutes? It seemed like I had a duty to challenge him and even offer some wisdom to him for his sake and his boys.

"Excuse me," I said in a polite yet serious tone. "Are you going to let the two boys come to blows?"

The man regarded me almost analytically, turned to get an update on the brawl, and then looked back to address me.

"Are you suggesting that I go down there? Do you think I should break it up?"

I was shocked that he was so oblivious to the obvious. "Yes! Of course, you should. You are encouraging violence!"

The man looked back at the boys as he considered my rebuke. Then he spoke. "If I go down there, a few things will happen, now and later. First, I will embarrass my son. Even at his age, he feels the need to be independent and would probably resent my intervention. Secondly, this will not be the first bully he encounters. If he doesn't learn how to deal with this level of adversity, how will he be prepared for the greater challenges of the future?"

"You speak as if you only care about one of your boys."

"Only one is my son. The other is the child of another."

Suddenly, the entire scene appeared much different from my initial assessment. My attitude toward the man was now one of respect. He was superior to me in knowledge and wisdom. Perhaps he could answer the newest question that my mind now presented.

"But what about the other boy?"

The man looked back at the two as a tinge of sadness crossed his face. "He is not my son. I supposed I could go over, physically remove him, even spank him. But how would that make me appear? How would it make you feel if you saw me doing that to your son? No. My primary concern has to be for my son, and this is what is best for him right now."

17. Reckless Driving

The hallway was sterile, an odd blend of grandiose and bland. The polished marble floor melded into the walls where green sconces cast light against a white ceiling. The bench where the two young people (no more than a boy and a girl, really) sat did nothing to warm up the space. It must have weighed a ton, appearing made from the same stone as the floor. The fact that the bench was cold underneath them only added to their sense of foreboding.

The youngsters had only been driving for a few months. From an early age, fear of police and courts had been ingrained into their minds.

"That policeman is going to get you if you don't wear your seatbelt!" their mothers would chide. Their fathers didn't help either, as they slammed on the brakes each time they saw a patrol car. Driving in constant fear can erase any enjoyment of the trip.

They had both been so excited to get their driving privileges. Having a driver's license felt like an open-ended ticket to freedom. Given the choice between the keys to the car or the keys to the city, they would have instantly chosen the car.

And now, through a combination of saved money, chores, and parental benevolence, each had their own set of wheels. It had been so liberating, pressing the pedals, turning the steering wheel, and choosing their own direction. But now, each one sat holding a speeding ticket in their hand as they waited to be led to the gallows.

They were similar in age and height. Perhaps the most notable difference was their body language. The boy, who we'll call Shaky, was perched on the edge of the bench. His legs were bouncing nervously as he unconsciously wrung his hands and looked anxiously down, awaiting his summons. The girl, called Poised, sat back with good posture. She was contemplative but far from apprehensive.

"What do you think they're gonna do to us?" Shaky whispered pitifully.

"That's a good question," Poised replied.

"I heard about this kid who had to go before the judge, and they made him do community service all summer. They made him wear one of those striped prison jumpsuits and everything."

Poised nodded.

Shaky continued, "And I heard about this other kid who owned a Camaro. The judge ordered that he give over his keys and that the car be sold. Can you believe it?"

Poised nodded. "Actually, I can."

"And this one guy had to go visit people in the hospital who had been injured in car crashes. I think he had to serve them food and help them walk around and stuff."

Poised answered, "Interesting."

"I don't see how you're not freaking out right now. Are you worried about what's gonna happen? Are you not a little scared of the judge?"

Poised turned. "I do fear the judge...but I'm not afraid of what he will do to me."

"I don't understand."

"The judge is my father."

"What? First of all, that's not fair. Second of all, how did you get a ticket in the first place? You'd think every cop in town would know your dad."

"That's actually why I got the ticket in the first place. How fast were you going?"

Shaky took advantage of a potentially sympathetic audience. "Well, first of all, the cops give you ten over. And then, the speed limit dropped to 35. I still thought it was 55. But then the cop said I was going 70, but my speedometer was only showing 68 when I saw his lights. He probably doesn't even calibrate his radar. You know, I should use that against him on the stand. He probably makes bad calls all the time."

"I was going 40 in a 35."

"Whoa! Talk about strict! Did you mouth off to the cop or something?"

"No, but it's like you said. Every cop in town knows my dad. And he told them sternly that I was not to receive any breaks, that if they caught me speeding, he wanted them to write me a ticket."

"Well, it's probably just a scare tactic. The judge will probably act really mean on the bench and then throw it out as soon as you leave."

"You obviously don't know my dad. He's had a habit of following the rules and making sure that I do, too. If it were up to me, I'd rather work to pay the fine and somehow leave him out of it. Unfortunately, that's not reality."

"So, what do you think he will do?"

"Well, he's always been very creative with his discipline. It's always been related to the offense, and it's always been for my good."

"For your good? Do you hear yourself right now?"

"My dad loves me. It didn't make sense when I was younger, but now I see that everything he's ever done has been for my good. I trust him even when I've messed up."

"But five over? Come on! Everyone goes at least five over."

"And, sadly, everyone is wrong. When we go up there, my dad is going to open the law book and read the speeding statute. It will say that anyone going over the posted speed limit is guilty. There is no mention of '10 over,' or '5 over,' or 'everybody does it'."

"So your dad is a real hard nose, huh?"

"No. He's actually kind and generous...and fun," she replied. "He doesn't always wear the robe. Sometimes, he takes it off, and he's just a normal guy. But think about his job. All day long, he sees people who've been hurt by careless drivers. I can't blame him for being strict."

There was silence between them.

"So, how do I get on good terms with your dad?"

18. Rejecting Life Rings

I t took a while for me to realize that I was in trouble. We bobbed up and down upon the unstable surface, an infinity of water in every direction. It was pretty decent. In fact, several elements of our situation were quite pleasurable. The sun was warm on our faces, and the blue of the mostly clear sky was pleasing to our eyes. Occasionally, seagulls would flap past and squawk noisily. We never could discern if they were scorning or encouraging us. But as time passed, we began to envy their ability to rise above our predicament and instinctively navigate back to a place of safety.

Some of us were more talkative than others. Some had faces twisted in consternation, unable to feel hope or pleasure because of their looming fate. On the other end of the spectrum were those who seemed oblivious to their peril. They trod water in a leisurely fashion and made it a point to appear as comfortable as possible. This was either a strong hope in deliverance...or in themselves. I paddled near one of these, a man just past his prime but still in excellent condition.

"Hello!" I offered cheerily.

A big smile. "Hello, yourself. Lovely day, isn't it?"

"Yes. It is quite nice. Have you heard any rumors of rescue?"

"Rescue? From what? We have the sunshine. The weather is beautiful. I've actually found some edible bits floating by in the water."

"I agree, but we're adrift on the ocean. We can't stay out here forever."

His face suddenly turned sour. "Who says? I'm in good shape. I bet you I could tread water for a week! I've got everything I need. I don't need rescue."

This was apparently a sensitive topic, but I pressed on. "But what about after this week? Surely, your arms and legs will grow tired. And the bits floating in the water are as unpredictable as the currents. Wouldn't you like to be rescued?"

His face was now stern, his jaw set and eyes narrow. He paused before he spoke. "No, I would not. If someone was aware of our predicament and left us like this, they would be horrible. No, there is no one. It is just us, and we do the best we can for as long as we can."

"But have you considered how we came to be in these circumstances? What if our actions caused us to be here? What if the time of day, the warmth of the sun, and the mysterious bits of food are all gracious offerings? What if we deserve even less?"

"My point exactly. If there is some sadistic being out there stringing us along, I don't want anything to do with it."

"I don't know. I think there might be more to the story. If rescue were available, I would avail myself of it."

"Fine—waste your life searching an empty horizon. But if your dream ship were to appear, I'd give them the finger."

With that, he turned around and began to console himself with what appeared to be more pieces of soggy bread. I continued to tread water as the morning became afternoon. At about 3:00, by my estimation, another treader drew near me.

Not a treader...but a floater! He had...a life ring! It was under his arms, and he was safely supported.

"Hello!" he offered.

"Where did you get that?" I know my greeting lacked courtesy, but I was amazed.

"Well, you get straight to the point. I like that. It means you want one too."

"Well, of course, but how? I see yours, but where did it come from? If you give me yours, how will you stay afloat?"

"Ahh. All good questions. Mine was given to me. The lady who gave me this life ring only had hers as well. When she offered it to me, I was reluctant to accept it. The arrangement was too strange. But she encouraged me to take it. She slid it off, held it out, and then nodded her approval. In a moment of desperation, I took hold of it, and hers was still safely in place, supporting her. It somehow replicated itself for me and remained hers as well. And now, I am following her example. I have yet to rid myself of this salvation." He smiled warmly with this last statement.

What did I have to lose? I held out my hands as he maneuvered his over his head and extended it toward me. I placed both hands on it and greedily slid both of my arms inside so that it surrounded me. His was still securely under his own arms! I don't know how. Our eyes met, and we shared a moment of mutual understanding. We had been saved! We were being saved! We would be saved! With the life ring's unfailing buoyancy, we knew we could weather the waves. I was overjoyed and held tightly to my source of hope. But as the sun moved closer to the horizon, I thought about my previous acquaintance and wondered how he was faring. With a sense of duty to my fellow man, I paddled back toward his position. He now looked fatigued. His face had lost confidence, and in its place was beleaguered anguish. He had been gathering bits of bread and had even pressed several of them together in what I assumed was his attempt to make a flotation device. The situation demanded gentleness.

"Hello again, friend. It's getting late. How are you doing?"

He turned and recognized me. He tried to force his expression to look positive, but his strained eyes and wrinkled face betrayed him. "Me? Oh, I'm fine. Just a few more pieces of bread and I should be able...." Even as he tried to compress the pieces, they became more saturated and less effective. He tried to position himself on the self-made raft, but it disintegrated beneath him. He grabbed at the tendrils of lost hope, but they began to sink ominously. I seized the moment.

"Friend, would you like a life ring?"

He considered me and my offer, reasonable thought fighting internal anger. "It may work for you, but I don't need it. Keep it to yourself...and leave me alone."

"But friend, you do need it...just as I do. It is free. The only thing keeping you from receiving it is your pride."

"My pride? Now you're criticizing me? Can't you see I'm struggling to stay afloat, and you console me with preaching?"

"So, you admit that you're struggling? That's good. I was, too. Trust me, this will help you weather the seas."

"I will not. I hate you, and I hate you for offering it. I hate whoever gave it to you. I am going to tread water and figure out a way to make something of this bread I have accumulated. Now, for the last time, leave me alone."

I knew I could not force a life ring on him. Perhaps someone else would come by before he slipped beneath the surface. But I would move on and offer my life ring to others. It truly was the gift that keeps on giving.

19. RIGHTS OF PASSAGE

Discovery of the ferries came with my newfound awareness of the river. Perhaps I had always known somewhere in the back of my mind that it existed, but its relevance until now had seemed negligible. The young hear stories of the river, but those stories usually come across as scare tactics or folklore. But the passage of time, a close call, or some other form of revelation brings us all to the brow of a hill from which we gain a panoramic view of its full width, depth, and turbidity. Its inky black waters pass by with total indifference. They are only slightly disturbed by the endless line of boats that sit beached along its nearby bank.

It seemed obvious that I should investigate each to see which offered perhaps the safest, the most pleasant, or even the fastest way across. On the other hand, their schedules would make one preferable over another, as a late departure is usually preferred in this case.

The first boat was the largest. It was ornate in its detail and painted a pristine white. The forecastle towered over the expansive decks and rigging. *Now, this is a ship that will take me safely to the other side.* I shouted to a deckhand who was wearing a smart, crisp uniform. His demeanor was serene, and he looked down at my position.

"Ahoy! Can I come aboard to meet the Captain? I would like to inquire about passage."

The deckhand stifled a frown and addressed my questions. "The Captain is not available to passengers. You might have the occasion to see him in the bridge through the glass, but it would be brief and distant."

"Oh. Is it important that I know the Captain? It would seem reasonable that he should have concern for me and that I be confident in him."

"His concern is for the ship, and the ship should be sufficient proof of his ability."

This made sense to me at the moment, and I asked again if I could come aboard.

The deckhand replied. "You are welcome to visit, but the possibility of passage requires extensive training and certification."

"Certification?"

"Yes," he said flatly. "We don't want any stowaways, freeloaders, or swindlers aboard. Nor do we care for reprobates, thieves, harlots, liars, brawlers, or people of lewd behavior."

I mentally reviewed the list and realized I had dabbled in several of these offenses.

"I don't consider myself any of those things, but an investigation into my past would reveal some evidence to the contrary."

The deckhand frowned at this confession.

"We have processes and procedures for passengers like you. You will learn them in the training, and IF you receive your certification, you can begin to observe them."

"I'm not opposed to that if that's what passage requires. But can I come aboard to see if I am capable of pursuing the training?"

The deckhand considered this and lowered the rope ladder. As I crawled over the gunwales, he instructed me not to touch anything or imitate anything I saw the other passengers doing. He reminded me that I was not yet certified. The dormitory and functional areas of the ship were even more impressive than the ship's exterior. I marveled at the cost of such a vessel. Hopefully, equal value had been given to the engine, prop, and structure.

As the deckhand escorted me around the main deck, I could not help but comment on the impeccable appearance of his livery. A question tumbled from my unguarded mouth.

"How do you keep your uniform so immaculate? I would have thought ship work would be grimier."

"Perhaps on the lesser vessels. We have taken great pains to avoid such pollution."

"And how is your ship so much larger than the others?" To be truthful, these surroundings had put me in a state of awe.

The deckhand replied almost defensively. "Because we own the exclusive rights for passage. None of the others have achieved this privilege, and their individual paltriness confirms their condemnation."

"Wow. And who is the issuing governance of these rights?"

With smugness, he answered. "We are."

As the tour concluded, he offered to schedule me for my first evolution of training. I thanked him warmly for his time but concluded that time may be of the essence. What if my departure was accelerated before training was completed? Perhaps one of the other ships might offer something a bit more straightforward.

As I walked to the second ship, disappointment crept into my gut. After visiting the first, all others would pale in comparison. I wish the first had been docked at the end of the line to serve as some sort of zenith.

The second ship was also very nice (albeit smaller and less regal). I asked a deckhand if I could come aboard, and he welcomed me warmly, even with an embrace. Immediately, I noticed jubilant music and saw passengers dancing about on the foredeck. Out of my peripheral vision, I thought I saw the deckhand of the first ship casting disapproving glances down at this festive and casual crowd.

My host asked me questions about my work and where I live with sincere interest. He offered me some refreshments (which really hit the spot) and highlighted several of the ship's amenities. Unlike the first tour, which seemed like a crucible, this seemed more like a sales pitch. The passengers were equally friendly, and some offered to teach me the dance that they were enjoying. It seemed harmless enough, and I found myself getting caught up in the emotion that had been created. I could see myself being friends with these people.

When I asked to see the Captain, the deckhand tapped a dancing man on his shoulder. He was amazingly normal and blended into the crowd. After identifying me as a visitor, he offered me refreshments and asked what I thought of the ship.

"It looks like lots of fun. What type of training do I need to gain passage?"

He laughed freely and said, "We'll teach you the basics, life jackets, safety drills, and dinner schedule, but the most important thing is group cohesiveness."

"Group cohesiveness? Why is that?"

Still smiling, he answered, "Because we are all on a journey. I am. You are. They are." he said as he motioned up to the deck of the first ship.

"So, do you own rights to passage as well? The first ship claimed they alone possessed them."

He laughed again as he continued to bob to the music. "You can't own rights to passage! It's a river. You cross it. It's what people do. Everyone will cross it."

"But does everyone cross it successfully?"

He slowed his swaying ever so slightly as he considered this. "How would I know? How would anyone know?"

I appreciated his honesty, but thoughts of my fate suddenly took precedence over considerations of comfort. "Your ship is pleasant and fun, but I would like more assurance before I settle in."

"The assurance comes with your acceptance. Acceptance that everyone can make his or her own choice about the passage. Look around. Any of these ships seem seaworthy. We'd love to have you on ours, but one's as good as the other."

This seemed unsettlingly ambiguous. The first captain had been aloof and unreachable. The second was oddly informal and nonchalant. I needed something in between. I thanked them for the visit and promised I would return, although it tasted like a lie even as it passed my teeth.

The third ship's crewman left me even more ambivalent. This one, too, claimed exclusive rights and was very critical of the previous two ships. The fourth had no engine but only rows of rowing positions. It seemed to require a lot of personal effort. The fifth had no captain or crew but an attitude that it would all somehow work out.

As I continued down the row of ships, hopelessness came over me. Then, I saw a house built on the shoreline overlooking the water. The house was dated in appearance, and a lack of maintenance revealed its age. A man sitting in a rocking chair on its porch shouted as I walked by.

"You're not actually considering getting on one of those things?"

It seemed obvious that I should, and I was puzzled that he did not think so.

"Of course. Why? Are you not?"

"Why should I? I was born on this shore. I have no assurance that the other shore is any better or even exists. For all we know, this could be an ocean. Do you know anyone that's been to or seen the other side?"

In all honesty, I had not.

He continued. "And what's so bad about this side? I'd live here forever if I could."

I looked behind him at the rapidly deteriorating exterior of his home. His face revealed a similar dilapidation.

"But, I don't think you can."

His expression hardened. "Then go on! Go find your ship and sail away to Neverland! You'll come to ruin just like the rest of us."

He continued his ranting as I stumbled away and tried to counter his arguments in my mind. I began to pass by ships without stopping. They consisted of ethnicities that were dissimilar to me. Some had entertainment that was too loud, whereas others were too subdued. Every other ship claimed "exclusive rights to passage" and had explanations for why the others did not.

My journey along the beach became a trudge. The two trails I left in the sand were indicative that I no longer had the strength or ambition to raise my feet. My eyes were locked only on the ground directly ahead of me. The cacophony of currents and concerts rang hollow in my ears. That's when I heard him.

"Hello, friend. You look lost."

I stopped dead in my tracks and exerted great effort to turn my head his way. It was a simple boat suitable for perhaps only two crew. Its sail hung neatly beside the mast, and the rudder was in a 'kicked up' position on the end of the tiller. Its sole occupant was a muscular yet amicable sailor. He wore clothes that bore marks of hard work and service. His eyes were kind and knowing. He sat in his little boat with a smile that invited conversation without pressure.

"I am."

He nodded. "That is an excellent place to start. I suppose you are concerned about the passage."

"Should I not be?"

"It's what's natural to a human. I can understand that."

His statement confused me: *Wasn't he human also?* I took a moment to examine his boat.

"Sir, I mean no offense, but your boat is the humblest of the fleet. What assurance can you give me of safe passage?"

He paused before he answered yet maintained direct eye contact with me. "You'd have to ask the others I've carried across."

My eyes widened. "You've been to the other side?"

He simply nodded, closing his eyes briefly.

"So, what certifications would I need to come aboard?"

"Well, that depends. Do you want to come aboard?"

"Yes!" I said eagerly. "I most certainly do."

"That alone will suffice."

"But what fees do you charge? The others have demanded money, ceremonies, and acts of penitence."

"Your company will be sufficient. In time, I hope that we might be friends."

His nature was quickly endearing itself to me.

"I don't understand. You seem to be the most qualified and capable, yet you ask the least. And you are also the last in line."

He slowly nodded again. "People usually find me most attractive when they've grown weary of all the rest."

"Well, shall we be going?" I asked as I began to throw one leg over the low bow.

He held his hand up and said, "Not yet."

I froze in the awkward pose and wondered what small print would be revealed.

"It's not your time. When it is, I'll be waiting here just for you."

I suddenly missed him even though we were still together. Time would pass between now and then. "But what do I do until then?"

"Stay here. Visit the other ships. Make friends with their passengers. Find those who are anxious and fatigued. Offer my services."

The benefits and consequences of this arrangement raced through my mind. "But what do you gain from all of this?"

In a way that I could relate to, he said, "To be chosen, preferred, and trusted is reward enough."

20. Roots

S peaking in the soothing drawl of a true southern gentleman, the storyteller muses, "The carrot and the stick. The preferred nose of snowmen. Peas and carrots. Perhaps the only thing more synonymous with carrots is a rabbit. You rarely see one without the other. Why? Because carrots grow low to the ground, right where a rabbit resides. They are easy to grasp between the paws, perfect for munching while sitting upright and looking out for wolves. And most importantly, they are delicious! It's not just the subtle sweetness but also the crisp texture and the loud crunch you hear when you snap off a bite with your two big front teeth! Yes, carrots may be the perfect food. The green leaves are not desirable, but they make good handles for pulling them out of the ground. Plus, they are like an "X" on a treasure map, and today I'm going treasure hunting.

"I guess you could say that I grew up on carrots. Like most memories, the olfactory and gustatory senses are the best catalysts for recalling life's sweetest moments. Just one bite into that beta carotene delight, my mind goes back to my childhood, hopping after my mother and watching her pull on the green leaves until that orangey goodness appeared. She was more practical with her consumption. She would sit on her haunches, lopping off mouth-sized pieces as she wearily scanned the horizon in all directions for coyotes or dogs. The endless variety of predators we had to keep an eye out for was a bit too much for me to remember, so I just called them "tail-waggers." When she heard me speak critically about our adversaries, she would remind me that I, too, had a tail. But mine didn't wag. Not really.

"With her around, it was easier for me to indulge in the scrumptious starch. She always seemed so jumpy and paranoid, which, in my naïve mind, detracted from our delectable dinner. We rabbits have keen eyesight, which helps us spot any troublemakers from a long way off. It's because our eyes are mounted high on our heads. And since we have an eye on each side, we can see almost 360 degrees around ourselves. Plus, we have more rods in our retinas than our human counterparts, so we can see better at night. Daytime, however, has some drawbacks. Because we have fewer cones, color differentiation can be a real problem. Blue and greens aren't too bad, but red can really be confusing. And please don't stand directly in front of me. The spacing of my eyes makes it hard to focus on things directly ahead.

"As I grew into a more mature and, might I say, debonair rabbit, I wanted a more dependable source of nutrition than what could be found by scavenging. Even with our keen sense of smell, carrots might be difficult to find depending on the rain, seasons, and my white furry compadres. We each tended to stake a claim on which territory we intended to harvest. And a visit from a friend would need to be in response to an invitation. It is the gentlemanly thing to do.

"Now, I could have just kept on visiting Farmer Johnson's farm. Still, he had become most inhospitable over the last several months. First, there was wire fencing that appeared seemingly overnight. Although we had to squeeze through a hole in the corner, it did provide a feeling of refuge and protection as we nibbled nocturnally. Then, there were the watchdogs (or tail-waggers, as I like to say). Even though the initial sight of them sent chills up and down my spine, I have come to the conclusion that those two are the dumbest, laziest, and least efficient killing machines on this planet. Fortunately for us, we plod along in complete silence. The carrot crunching could be an issue, but ordering them to-go easily solves this dilemma.

"But lately, he had incorporated a thunder stick of sorts. First, Farmer Johnson looks out of his window late at night. Then, there is an angry monologue as he stomps downstairs and opens the door. Then he points that stick in our direction, and the most disturbing commotions come out of the end. It sounds like thunder! Somehow, it makes the ground around us shoot up into the air and strips the bark off the trees just over our heads. Whatever that dastardly device is intended for, it does not make us feel very welcome.

"Hence, the seeds. Now, this happened over time by trial and error. And most interestingly, the key factor was time. You see, carrots have a two-year life cycle. And in the second year, tiny flowers grow out of the leaves. Now, it happened by chance that some old, dried carrot flowers that I had noticed were covered up one night by the digging of a tail-wagger. At first, I was irritated that those Neanderthals had so clumsily covered over something so pleasing to the eye. But in just a few weeks, I began to see an even sweeter image appear from that dark mound of soil. Carrots! With this new knowledge, all I had to do was collect the oldest carrot flowers I could find, bury them in some secret location, and then bide my time.

"Having infinite access to carrots made me somewhat popular in the hare community, especially with the ladies. Like a king of carrots, you could almost say I had a hare-em! Harvesting my crop was hard work, but the profits of those pointy provisions made me a wealthy rabbit. It seemed like the world was my oyster, er...I mean, my carrot.

"One day, when all was right with the world, I went to prospect my next batch of orange gold. The time of year was right, and the leaves were the correct size. But imagine my surprise and dismay when I pulled the first one up and discovered a red ball! This made no sense. It was the wrong shape. It was the wrong color. Tentatively, I took a tiny bite. YUCK! This was no carrot. This was an imposter! I sat there, truly befuddled and confused. What on Earth had happened to my crop? Maybe it was just a fluke, so I pulled up the next one. Ahhh. This one was exactly as it should be. A fine specimen. But the next was another red, round ball. The next hour was full of frustration and dismay. About half of my harvest was not what it should have been.

"That night, I was truly vexed by this situation. I still had more than enough carrots for me and my customers. Still, these disgusting intruders were interfering with my industry, which affected my income, which affected my status. Mama would know what to do.

"I took one of these vile fruits of hades to her the next time I visited. I laid it down at her paws and gave her a look that implied, *I demand an explanation for this unfairness of life that you have neglected to warn me of!*

And with her usual patience, Mama said, "Did we not find radishes all the time when you were just a little ball of fur?" Her amused grin and nonchalance were infuriating. "You learn to recognize them a little better over time, but they still come up all the same."

"But I don't remember eating any radishes," I replied.

"Of course not, silly. I was protecting you from something

unpleasant just like I was always watching for someone dangerous."

"I sat silent as I contemplated this revelation. Mama had been watching out for me. I just hadn't been paying attention. I hugged her closely as we concluded our visit.

"The radishes continued to plague me. They were eating into my business and began to cast a shadow on my countenance. I had developed a phobia of pulling any carrot because of its potential to be something I did not want. No longer was I enthusiastically extracting my bounty. Now, each pull was accompanied by a dread of seeing that menacing crimson sphere.

"In a short time, the anxiety of the unknown began to compete with my drive to succeed. I became despondent. But when you have a lot of money, you begin to think money can fix any problem. I made some arrangements to have carrots shipped to my door. This would fulfill my caloric needs while sparing me the rude intrusion of radishes.

"The next day, there was a knock on my door. I opened it to find a simple cardboard box with my name written neatly across its top.

"*How delightful*, I said to myself. I opened the package, which held six long, delicious-looking carrots. Now, this was the life. I sat in my lair that evening, snacking and reflecting on how changes can be for the better. It seemed that my blues were being replaced by blue skies.

"Later that week, there was another knock on my door. There again was a package, but it was not sealed. It looked like it had been tampered with. My heart thumped with a dreadful hollowness as I took the package inside to examine its contents. Someone had eaten half of my carrots! How could this be? The harbor of my harvesting alternative was no longer safe.

"I contacted the delivery service and demanded that the

packages be taped and sealed. I refused to pay for a delivery that had been unsealed. They were very apologetic and said that this problem would be rectified immediately.

"I sat stewing the whole next morning. The expectation of incompetence from everyone was forming in my mind. The knock was heard, the package was delivered, and it showed no signs of tampering. With only surface-level relief, I took it inside and began to break the seal. So far, so good. As I opened the flaps, I saw the reassuring green leaves, which led down to a bundle of red circular devil fruit. I quickly closed the flaps and looked up in horror. Fear gripped me as every avenue of sustenance seemed destined to be ruined. I could not harvest only carrots. I could not have them safely delivered. And I could never, ever learn to enjoy, appreciate, or even tolerate radishes. Why did they even exist?

"I spent the next few days in a catatonic stupor. The daily knocks on the door competed with the growling of my hungry stomach. Indeed, packages were beginning to pile up outside, which must have concerned the deliverer. But no one checked on my well-being. My own mother was out of town visiting her ailing sister in the valley glade. She seemed very selfish for doing this in my present state of mind.

"What was a rabbit to do? Neither my cleverness nor my success could shield me from the bane of radishes. They seemed to me an inescapable nuisance, a thorn in my fur-covered flesh. I forfeited the next five days of my life brewing and stewing over this injustice.

"Hunger can be a powerful motivator. Equal to my craving for carrots was my longing for belonging. I missed being desired. I missed being needed. I missed being useful. I even missed the invisible visits from my delivery boy, inept as he may be. A crossroads was reached in my mind, with only one avenue seeming viable. And as life demanded, it was the hard one.

"It took time to gather a new bundle of dried carrot flowers. Finding a plot of fertile soil that would be difficult for someone to stumble across was more challenging. With an odd blend of despair and desperation, I began to reap both the carrots and the radishes. The radishes continued to disgust me and threatened to fracture my new and delicate resolve. But then I discovered that our neighbors to the north, the deer and squirrels, not only tolerated the round, red scourges but somehow preferred them! Being the good salesman I am, I did not question their dietary madness. It even seemed good for business for them to see me nibbling on one as they arrived to shop. Perhaps even the most unappetizing intrusions in our lives can develop value."

21. Stay of Execution

He would give them nothing. They could starve him, beat him, lock him in a dark cell, but—nothing. He would not give one inch, not one shred of information. He would remain loyal at all costs.

The chains seemed excessive. Edward had chains around his wrists, ankles, neck, and waist. They were draped around his drooped shoulders and dragged on the floor behind him as he walked. But Edward would endure them. He would not show weakness. He knew the interrogation was imminent, so he continued to strengthen his own resolve.

He knew from stories that their commander was a ruthless tyrant. He had been responsible for events of savagery that could never be justified. Oh, if only he had some hidden weapon at his disposal. He fantasized about what that might look like. The guards would drag him before the commander and shove him down at his feet. The commander would undoubtedly be sitting smugly behind some large table or perhaps behind some intimidating perch like a judge's bench. They would do everything they could to humiliate him. He would play the part and grovel on his knees so he could get close enough to strike. And when they had let their guard down, he would pull the weapon from his waist and strike the death blow. It would be a glorious (and probably suicidal) victory.

Time went by, allowing his anger to steep. It brewed and became darker like a rich tea. When the fateful meeting finally occurred, Edward wanted to be mentally prepared to meet the enemy.

And then, a door opened. There was warm light coming from the other side. Edward waited for the brutish guards to burst into his cell, but they never did. After a minute or so, curiosity won out, and he slowly moved toward the doorway to investigate. Was this a chance for escape? Was this a trap? Either possibility required caution. He slowly moved toward the doorway, his noisy chains ruining any hope for stealth. As he neared, he peered around the edge to see what lay beyond. It was a simple room with two chairs. A man about his own age sat in one. The man wore no uniform. Who was he? Undoubtedly, an agent. But his clothes were unimpressive. Could he be another prisoner? Edward thought *one cell is as good as another*, and he moved into the next room. The man stood, smiled, and gestured to the other chair with his hand. *Stay focused. Do not give them anything*, he silently reminded himself.

"Please, have a seat," the other man proffered politely.

Edward approached but decided to stand in an act of defiance. He proudly held his chin up and averted his gaze, preferring to stare at some distant speck on the far wall.

"Suit yourself, but I think you will be much more comfortable sitting down. I'm sure your chains are burdensome."

Was that sarcasm? The tone wasn't sarcastic. This must be psychological warfare. He continued to stand rigidly at attention. A minute went by, and the other man patiently stood there, his expression almost pleasant. By the second minute, Edward began to feel foolish. This was not the inquisition he'd pictured in his imagination. He caved ever so slightly, relaxing his posture and glancing at the chair.

The other man gestured again and said "Please," as he took the other seat.

Begrudgingly, Edward sat down but scowled so that no one would doubt his fortitude. "Would you care for something to drink? Something to eat?" the other man offered.

Silence.

"If you'd like, you can get cleaned up. We have comfortable clothes you can wear."

He lifted his wrists to indicate the chains and contorted his face to convey how foolish the offer was.

"Ah, yes. Your chains. Well, the offer stands if you change your mind."

Edward sat stoically. They were trying to butter him up, but he would not be softened.

"So, I'm sure you have something you would like to tell me."

He was a stone. His lips would not part. They would get nothing.

"I don't mean about your side or your purpose. I mean about me."

What kind of tactic was this? He had not prepared himself for mind games. Where was this leading?

Edward deliberated over speaking to this man. Sure, they had dressed his interrogator in simple clothes and removed the guards to put him at ease, but they could not be trusted. They were all two-faced, diabolical fiends. The silence continued.

"Look. You're obviously puzzled about all of this and very leery, so I will tell you who I am. Then you can tell what you think of me. I am your enemy. You've grown up hearing stories about my father."

This was him! Edward thought as his eyes involuntarily widened. He wished with all his might that a knife or shank would somehow appear in his hand. He could strike a blow for his people and strike a blow to the commander at the same time. To be so close to opportunity and so helpless was frustrating beyond words. He briefly thought about lunging at the stranger. Still, the calmness Edward saw in him said volumes about his abilities in warfare. Plus, there were these vexatious chains.

Edward's anger boiled over, and he spoke. "You are the son of a tyrant! Your father is wicked, and I'm sure the apple does not fall far from the tree! If your father was here, I would spit in his face." The statement gave him an idea, and he reacted on instinct. "Ptooey!" The spittle flew through the air and landed on the other man's forehead and cheeks. This was the moment when he would be beaten by this man or the guards. Edward flinched and braced himself for an assault...which never came. No guards rushed in. No clubs struck his head. After a moment, he let his eyes crack open and lowered his hands, which had been held up in defense. The stranger was wiping his face with a handkerchief and had a very sorrowful expression. Then something very unsettling happened. A small bowl full of liquid was beside the man's chair. Edward was sure it had not been there before. The man took the same handkerchief, dipped it in the water, and leaned toward him.

This was it! The liquid was undoubtedly Chloroform or maybe Sodium Pentothal. Once they covered his mouth and nose, he would lose consciousness or (equally scary) his defiant spirit. The handkerchief moved closer to his face, and he strained under the chains to keep his distance. They had now grown even heavier and were holding him in place in the chair. The cloth was inches from him, and he turned his head away to buy a few more precious seconds. Then, the cloth touched his forehead. He winced and reclosed his eyes. But there was no odd odor. It was cool on his skin, and it felt agreeable. The cloth wiped down his temples, his nose, his cheeks, and his chin. As he sat there with fists clenched and eyes closed, he could hear the man wringing out the rag and then felt it returning to his wrist, arms, and hands. It was the first sensation of relief he had experienced since he couldn't remember when. The feeling became immense and spread throughout his body. It felt like liquid Valium. The tension and the anger began to dissipate, and Edward felt his limbs relax. He sank into the chair as the man cleaned his shins, ankles, and feet. The weight of the chains was somehow more tolerable and lighter than before. He still felt their weight in the areas where the metal touched, but comfort had suffused elsewhere. He slowly opened his eyes and tried to comprehend his new mental state.

If the bowl had contained some chemical, it had been effective. Edward viewed the stranger differently now. Where was his hatred, the vehemence he'd worked so hard to maintain?

The man looked passive and said, "Shall we start again?"

Edward nodded dumbly.

"So, what would you like to tell me?"

He had practiced his insulting speech many times, and the right words came out...but were strangely devoid of malice. They were calm and reasonable. "I always thought you were awful. I'd heard about the death and destruction your family was responsible for, and it made you monsters in my eyes. I... hated you."

"Ahhh. Honesty. Now we're getting somewhere." The stranger smiled and leaned back in his chair. "Please, continue."

"My people—we did everything we could to defy you. We vilified anything we heard that was affiliated with you, good or bad. We twisted every report to cast you in a negative light and did our best to sway others away from you."

The man nodded in understanding. "I see." He paused in thought. "Let me ask you a question. Suppose you witnessed a large man striking a child on the back repeatedly. The child's face was a mask of anguish and fear. You run over to intervene, and upon closer inspection, you see that the child is choking and that the man is trying to clear his breathing passage. Would you admit that you saw the situation incorrectly?"

"Well, I...," Edward stammered.

"Imagine that you had a deadly, aggressive tumor growing in your body, and I was the surgeon. Would you ask me to cut you open and remove it? Would you want me to leave half of it behind? Any part of it?"

Silence.

"Some situations require more explanation, wouldn't you agree?"

Edward nodded dumbly once again. But the wheels of logic continued to spin in his mind, and he countered with another accusatory question. "OK, so you can explain away the harmful things you've done. Maybe you have your reasons. But what about the things you haven't done, the things you've neglected? One of our biggest complaints is the suffering that you turn a blind eye to."

"Interesting. So, you and your people see me as a villain and expect me to be a philanthropist simultaneously."

"We know that you have power and resources. We've heard what you're capable of. We just don't think you're doing a very good job."

"Let me give you another scenario. Imagine someone going on a shooting spree. Several people died, and the police had the gunman cornered. He's not giving up and will kill more people if he is not shot. What would be the reasonable response?"

"Obviously, to remove the threat to innocent people."

"What if the gunman was your son? What if the gunman was you?"

"But I would never! My son would never do such a...," but an answer for the scenario was still expected. "I don't know."

"Evil exists on a spectrum. People view murder as being on the far end of that spectrum and tend to feel good about themselves because they are nowhere near that point. But as they make that assessment, they themselves reside on that same spectrum. Who has not stolen something, even if only something small? Who has not lied? Who has not felt superior to someone else? Who has not wanted revenge? If someone was responsible for correcting all of the evil on that spectrum, where would they draw the line? Would the jaywalkers get a free pass? How about the vandals? The petty thieves? How about the rapists? The stalkers? The fantasizers? Who draws the line? How close to that line are you? If we were to extinguish all evil, would you be exempt?"

The prisoner's expression became sullen as he wrestled with these impossible dilemmas. "Well, what about these chains? What about this prison? You clean me up and pretend to be kind, but look at me! How can you pretend to be good and let me stay like this?"

The angry questions hung in the air. The man's eyes remained fixed on his own. "Those are not our chains."

It couldn't be true. When one makes a serious accusation, the last thing one wants is for it to be disproven. Edward's eyes moved down to his wrists, where he took a closer look at the shackles. His stomach sank as he recognized the design. They were his own.

He had not manufactured them, but they were from his people, society, and way of life. Suddenly, he recalled the path to where he now found himself. He remembered attaching himself to things and ideas throughout the years. He remembered devoting himself to pursuits while ignoring or accepting their costs. He remembered the weight of those chains pulling him down into a dark pit, which became his cell. There, he assembled the arguments that would place the blame for his dilemma on a shared enemy.

"I came down into the pit because I feel pity for you. I feel concern for you. Your life would be so much more fulfilling without them, living under the light of the sun and breathing in fresh air."

Edward's heart was beating wildly. This was too much to comprehend all at once. Could he have been wrong all of these years? Could he really be responsible for his own pain and confinement? Who was this man sitting across from him now?

"But how? How can I be free?" He lifted his wrists as a beggar would, indicating that he has nothing but needs everything.

"Open your hands."

He looked down and was surprised to see his hands clenched around the chains. The muscles in his forearms were straining to maintain their grasp, and the fingers seemed locked into place. He tried to mentally pry them open, but a wave of fear washed over him. Did these chains not provide some comfort? Didn't they offer some certainty? He had worn them for so long.

The stranger's hands slid over Edward's and slowly opened the cramped fingers. As the chains began falling away, the other man took them and placed them in his own lap. Edward, feeling a newfound mobility and lightness, began to unbind himself. He pulled shackles from his ankles and removed the collar from his neck. He slung off heavy chains from his shoulders and leaped up from the chair with joy. Willing hands continued to receive the tarnished restraints. Edward thrust his hands into the air and gazed with wonder at the absence of handcuffs. He never wanted to go back. He looked down at the stranger who sat with a pile of rusty, dirty chains gathered in his arms. The stranger smiled and said, "You are free."

But what now? If chains could be removed so easily, what about this cell? Was there any reason for him to remain in the darkness? "I want to see the light."

The stranger nodded his assent and said, "This is good. You've seen what magnitude of deliverance can take place by moving toward the light of the doorway. Imagine what waits beyond."

And with those words, Edward began to look for the source of light.

22. Stolen TV

"What the...? Dude! Somebody took our TV!"

Frank and Tony stood in the small room and looked about at the messy surroundings that had somehow been made worse by the break-in. The carpet near the window glistened with thousands of tiny shards of broken glass. The low coffee table near the wall had a thin layer of dust except where the base of the flat-screen TV normally sat. The wires and plugs from their video console now lay helplessly unattached.

Their mouths were wide open. In their hearts was a mixture of incredulity, fear, and anger. Incredulity because no one really expects disaster. Fear because the thieves might still be close by or might come back. After all, there was now a big, open hole where the window used to be. The anger was because something important had been taken from them. It had value. It was useful. It provided a high level of entertainment for them. Untold hours were spent gazing hypnotically at its screen as thumbs and fingers moved deftly over game controllers.

"So now what?"

Frank, the more impetuous of the two, responded. "We call

the cops! That's what." He plucked his cell phone from his pocket and was dialing 9 1 1 when Tony grabbed his hand.

"Wait a second." His mind was analyzing why this seemed like a bad idea. "What if the cop comes in here and sees all our other stuff? Any other day, we'd never let one in here."

"But we're the victims, dude!" Frank interjected. "Somebody broke into our place and took our TV! That's, like, breaking and entering! They need to dust for prints and take, like, DNA samples and stuff."

"OK, but what about when they see our marijuana?"

Both young men dumbly looked at the table, the couch cushions, and the floor. The odor of the weed was pungent even though it did not immediately register in their nostrils.

"You think they'd make a big deal about that?"

"Are you serious? They're cops! It's what they do. They'd probably care more about the weed than our TV!"

"Oh, man. You're probably right."

They spent the next 20 minutes picking up seeds and bits of leaves. They saturated everything with air freshener, which gave the place the fragrance of a cotton candy machine blended with a reggae concert. Anyone who stepped foot inside would have instantly detected the effort to mask the obvious.

"Alright, let's call 'em," Frank insisted.

Tony grabbed his arm again. "Wait. What about the beer?" Their heads collectively turned toward the kitchen area and the fridge. Several dark, empty bottles and dented cans were scattered about the various surfaces. "Dude, we're only 20. We can't have that stuff here."

For another twenty minutes, they picked up bottles and took the half case in the fridge to their neighbor. They asked him not to drink any, and he said he'd gladly hold it for them. However, Frank and Tony both swore they heard the unmistakable click and hiss of a can being opened as their neighbor shut the door. They returned to their apartment and used more air spray.

"Alright, let's call 'em." Frank raised the phone and began to tap the numbers. Again, Tony's hand shot out and stopped him just in time.

"Wait! What about the merchandise?"

Hmmm. This was also a problem. Not everything in their bachelor pad had been purchased legitimately. Some things had been reappropriated when their former owners had not secured them well enough. There was the Bluetooth speaker, the scooter, the cooler, and what else? The bicycle which suspiciously missing its front wheel. Maybe they could stack it all in the closet.

For another twenty minutes, they went around the place trying to remember what was truly theirs and what was probably listed down at the station as stolen.

It had been unintentional, but the place actually looked almost presentable. They both scanned their formerly disreputable domicile and agreed that they could finally make the call. Ten minutes later, an officer knocked on their door. They opened it and thanked him for coming. He wrinkled his nose and cast them a sideways glance. He clicked his pen and began to jot down their information on his report. As they gave him their names as the victims, he followed protocol and forwarded them to dispatch. Two minutes later, the officer was applying handcuffs to both of them for unpaid traffic tickets. This seemed a horrible injustice to them.

"Man, we thought you were here to protect and to serve! We were robbed, and you're throwing us in jail? You should be out looking for the actual bad guys."

Their TV had ended up in a nearby apartment much like their own. And their neighbor watched his favorite show on it while enjoying another can of free beer.

23. Tarantula

I feel pretty good today, I thought as I brushed my teeth. This was my daily moment to evaluate my physical health as well as my emotional, mental, and spiritual welfare. Staring at myself in the mirror with a foamy mouth like that of a rabid dog allowed me to see a candid version of myself. *I need maintenance. I did not wake up perfect. Other people, like me, are also doing the best they can.* These and other thoughts percolated through my mind. *"But why do I feel particularly good today?"* I asked myself. I went through a mental to-do list, and they were all desultory tasks. *But wait. I'm meeting Janeen today!* Janeen is one of my favorite people. So smart and witty and funny.

When she laughs, I cannot help but smile. I could give you a hundred reasons why I like Janeen, but I could also sum it up with just one. Chemistry. We have that unspoken bond that can immediately unite total strangers in a chance meeting. I trust her. For a hundred reasons and simply for how she looks me in the eye. I see good in her. As I rinse and spit, I think of Janeen possibly performing the same hygiene chore at this very moment. She is human, too.

The morning goes by, and I'm on schedule. The things I could do on my list are done, and my mind is free to enjoy the prospect of my lunch date with Janeen. I get to the coffee shop five minutes early, but she is already there, sitting at a small round table in the corner. I receive a huge smile when she sees me, and it feels like a hug. I hold up my finger, asking her for a moment while I order my meal. It is delivered on a tray, and I go to greet my friend. She stands. We embrace briefly. We sit and wait for one of us to start with the volley of questions, answers, and stories that constitute conversation.

"So, how has your week been?" Janeen asks. She's so considerate. She listens attentively as I tell her. Her eyes register and respond to the various vagaries of my life's events. She nods. She flinches. She smiles. She empathizes at all the proper moments to let me know that she cares.

I go on for over five minutes when I begin to feel that it's time to reciprocate. Good conversation and true friendship require it. "Well, what about yours? How did the interview go?" Because I am a good friend, I am aware of important things in Janeen's life and give her opportunities to tell me about them.

Janeen is a wonderful storyteller. She asks a question or makes a statement that draws you into her situation. She provides details that paint pictures in your mind as if you were there. Her words have a flow that carries you from moment to moment. I was deeply engrossed in her narrative when I saw a dark spot moving in my peripheral vision. My eyes involuntarily broke contact for a moment to investigate. *Was that? A spider?* I looked back and nodded to affirm interest. *That was a spider, right? But it was big. Bigger than household spiders.* When Janeen's eyes rolled to describe a particularly challenging situation, I snuck another look. My heart stopped for a second. It was a tarantula...on the shelf beside her seat. *What was a tarantula doing in our coffee shop? Were they indigenous to our area?* I opened my mouth to warn Janeen, but her story began to crescendo. My eyes darted from Janeen to the spider, from Janeen to the spider. I lifted my hand from the table to get her attention. Janeen looked at my interruption and frowned slightly. Her story continued.

I parted my lips to indicate I needed to interject, but she parried with hand motions and sound effects. "Janeen, I... you need to... there's a..." But Janeen's increased volume was now attracting the attention of other diners.

The spider was crawling up her blouse and making its way up her back. Janeen's words were now muffled static in my ears. My friend was in potential danger. No, this was definitely dangerous. "Janeen!"

She stopped and fixed me with a stern gaze. "You know, I listened to your story without interrupting. And even though you've told me twice already about your lethargic goldfish, I still paid attention. Now, can I please finish my story?" Janeen was surprisingly ruffled.

I forced my eyes to lock onto hers and bared both rows of my teeth in a forced smile. *There it was! It was now cresting the back of her shoulder and making its way toward her neck. Should I swat it? What if I get bitten?* My eyes are pulled to the right, and I point at the silent assassin. "Janeen, there's a..."

Janeen holds her hands up like stop signs. "You know, our relationship is completely one-sided. It seems like I give you my time and attention, and you just nitpick little things about me. Do you know how difficult that is for me?"

I make a desperate attempt to protect her feelings and still warn her of this imminent threat. "You're absolutely right, it's just you have a..."

Janeen explodes. "There you go again! I seriously cannot believe you right now." The spider slides over her collar and disappears down her neckline.

I shiver. "But Janeen, you're my friend and I..." My words are frantic. Janeen stands up, slings her purse over her shoulder, and walks out of the café without saying goodbye. The hanging bell rings as the door opens and closes. "...just wanted to tell you that there's a spider in your shirt."

24. THE COMMANDER

As I drove to my next interview, I reviewed my strategy in my head, itemizing each issue and complaint. *OK. So, this guy is a military commander. He's probably one of those muscle heads who plows through problems without considering consequences. When I toured his base last week, it was absolute chaos; hardly anyone was wearing their uniform. Trash and vandalism were everywhere. There were fist fights, bad language, and just plain poor treatment. Most of the flags and emblems had been removed or defaced. Instead of discipline and order, there was only confusion and mayhem. Some commander! He must either be asleep at the wheel or so full of himself that he doesn't care about his troops. I will put him into a position where he can brag about himself and build up his ego before I kick the ladder out from underneath him.* Although I would never admit this, I loved seeing the mighty fall. I also loved being the one who caused it.

As I pulled into the address given, it was not what I expected. It was one of those World-War-II-style Quonset huts with simple white rock landscaping and the obligatory flag flying outside on a simple flagpole. There were no barbed wire fences or guards, just a screen in front of a plain wooden door. I thought it was odd that the door had no lock. I straightened my tie and checked the batteries on my recorder once more before knocking. After hearing footsteps, the door opened to a man about my own age wearing casual clothes that made mine look regal in comparison. He was slender but well-proportioned, warm but still professional. Obviously, an assistant or maybe an intern.

"Come in! Come in! I'm so glad you could make it." He led me toward an unimpressive wood desk with two wooden chairs in front. He rotated one toward me and offered it before sitting down in the other. He faced me, smiled, and clasped his hands in his lap.

Odd that he would wait beside me ,but I decided to use this time to prepare. I placed my recorder on the desk and checked the batteries once again. I took out my notepad, clicked my pen, and looked around the space. Perhaps the commander was finishing up another meeting, or maybe he was intentionally being late. It was a tactic that executives sometimes used to indicate that their time was more valuable than yours. I realized the intern was still facing me and waiting expectantly. It was getting awkward, so I decided to throw this guy a bone. "So, how long have you worked for the commander?"

"Well, it feels like an eternity!" He laughed at his own joke. "But, more accurately, I work with him. You could almost say we're one and the same."

Wow! This was certainly the most bold and self-elevated intern I'd ever met. I hope the commander wasn't as deluded as his staff. Mental instability could be a good angle for my article. "So, does the commander view you as an equal, or would he be OK with you assuming his authority?"

"Actually, he has given me all the authority. It's actually better this way."

I couldn't believe this guy. Did he expect me to believe he had any say-so anywhere? This guy wasn't impressive. This guy looked like he should be fetching coffee. I decided to call his bluff. "So, you're telling me that you, an assistant, could waltz onto the base, which is a complete trainwreck, by the way, and start bossing soldiers around?" I laughed out loud to emphasize my incredulity. This putz had it coming.

Then his smile morphed into something much less approving. "You did come here to interview the commander, yes? I expected you to be a little more cordial and courteous."

My mind rapidly began to contemplate insane possibilities. Had I somehow found myself on thin ice? Surely, I could not have misread the situation so completely. "Are you telling me that you are the commander?"

"I am."

"You're the one who has never lost a battle? You're the conqueror with limitless resources and power? You're the one who presumably has infallible insight into your enemy's intelligence?" My sarcasm had become blatant and downright rude. But I had committed myself to this course. "I just can't believe you expect me to believe you're the commander. I thought you were the intern."

"Lots of people make that mistake. How would you be more comfortable? With me in full display of my power? A parade with all of my troops? Perhaps I should be actively slaying my opponents. Would that be a proper setting for an interview?"

Wow. This guy was surprisingly grounded, articulate, and reasonable. Was I on some funny TV show? Were there hidden cameras somewhere? The idea that this guy was the one I'd heard so many glorious stories about was...absurd. I sat there stupefied, uncertain of how to proceed. I had prepared to set him up and watch him fall. Had he caused me to stumble into my own trap? I suddenly felt horribly uncertain, lost, and even afraid. The commander's eyes were on me. They were not angry, but they did not excuse me either.

"Shall we start over? It's what I would prefer," he said.

I sat there dumbly, weighing my options. I could continue insulting the man. I could grab my things and run out. But what about my future? People were expecting me to discover and reveal the truth. No. I couldn't leave here like this. Feeling like a very young child, I shyly pressed the record button on my recorder, clicked my pen, and propped my notebook up on my crossed knee. The humility that escaped my mouth surprised even me. "Forgive me. I'm ready."

The atmosphere immediately changed. The tension I had caused was somehow sucked out of the room and replaced with a sense of peace and acceptance? If he felt insulted, he did not show it. The smile was back, and he continued to sit there patiently with his hands clasped.

"So...I, uhh. So...you are the...commander." I stupidly wrote the word down in my notepad. I felt like one of those defense attorneys who scribbles on his legal pad to look engaged.

"Look. I'm sure you have some weighty questions you'd really like to ask me. As you've seen, I am not prone to rashness or intemperance. Ask what you'd like. Your absolute honesty would be appreciated."

So, this must be what my victims feel like when I expose them and trap them in a corner. It's not a good feeling. And just like them, any deception I had constructed was now laid bare. "I went to your base. It was a disaster. A complete disaster. Anyone who saw that would question your leadership. Soldiers were fighting, tearing up the place just out of spite, ignoring and defying anything that you would expect a soldier to do. The place was dirty and in disrepair. It seemed to be doing more harm than good. What am I supposed to think when I see something like that with my own eyes?"

"Excellent questions. And your observations are 100% accurate. So, how would you handle the situation if you were in my position?"

Hmmm. *It was nice of him to consider my opinion.* "Well...I guess if I truly had unlimited power and resources, I'd go in and clean house. I'd arrest all those rebels, lock them in prison, bulldoze the whole place, and start over."

"Interesting. And let me add one complication. What if one of your loved ones was also serving on the base? They could be the best or the worst of them. Your choice. Would you still flatten the place?"

I twisted uncomfortably in my seat. "Well... I'd. Well, I could go in ahead of time and get them out."

"And when you retrieve them, they tell you they don't want to go with you. They prefer life on the base. They're not interested in a different existence."

"But they wouldn't do that," I responded. "They would see that I have their best interest at heart. They would see that I care about them and that I'm trying to get them out of a dangerous situation."

"Is that how you saw me?"

The question stung. He had warmly welcomed me. Offered me a seat and made me comfortable. And what was my natural response? I was rude and accusatory. *What is wrong with me?*

"I'm trying to illustrate that the situation is not as simple as it sounds. The condition of the base is due to an enemy. They welcomed him and decided to follow him instead of me. His influence has caused what you have seen, and it causes them to be unreasonably hostile toward me. Their treason should have been punishable by death, but that's not my way. My knee-jerk reaction is heartache and compassion. Heartache for the consequences of their decision and compassion because these soldiers have value. A lot has been put into them. They have the potential to provide amazing service to me and each other."

"So why not just kill the enemy? Show them who's boss and wrap up this whole confusing mess."

"They are drawn to his ways and what he offers. It's like a sickness or an addiction. If I kill their leader, they would not view it as salvation. No. They would have to see the situation and their condition clearly before they would appreciate that."

"In your scenario, it seems impossible. People need rescue, but they don't want it. If you go in now and clean house, they get caught up in the judgment. But you have to do something!"

He leaned forward in his chair. "That's right! And I have a plan."

I positioned my pen over my notepad to capture what he considered juicy.

"I'm sneaking onto the base."

Deflation. That's all I felt. Maybe I was right after all. This man was insane.

"Why would you sneak onto your own base? That makes no sense! You should come busting through the gates in a tank or something."

"Did you not just hear the complexities of this situation? They will not respond to that. They will be angry or afraid. No. I will take my place in their ranks, exercise, run, and eat in the mess hall. I will win over one. Then we will win over two. Then we will win over four, and the growth will be exponential."

"That sounds crazy and hopeless."

"Perhaps. But it gives people a chance. You've met me. You've spent time with me. What qualities would you ascribe to me now that you've gotten to know me?"

I shrugged. "Reasonable? Patient? Considerate? Caring?"

"And you would be correct. But now I would like to include you in my plan. Would you go with me?"

"What?" My mouth fell open. "Why? What makes me qualified? Why would I go into that dump and risk getting beaten up?"

"Do you remember your solution to the chaos?"

"Yeah. The roundup, the prison, the bulldozer."

"Well, that ultimately will be the solution to the base's problem. But I want to rescue as many as will accept me. I cannot be who I am and allow it to continue forever. I am incredibly patient, but even I have my limits."

25. The Enlarging Pit

J ared could not believe it was in stock. He had wanted one for so long and barely had enough money. But today was the day. He swallowed, pushed down the nagging doubts about the purchase, and reached for his wallet.

As he walked home, he held the bag carefully with both hands just above waist level. In addition to being very expensive, it was also contraband, not so much in the legal sense but in the marital sense. Jared and his wife had an unspoken rule that they discussed any purchases over $50. This had been more than that, twice as much, actually, and he had not "cleared" it with her. But Jared worked. He had income. He was his own man. Right? As he neared his home, he suddenly felt exposed and guilty.

"Phew!" Thankfully, his wife's car was not in the driveway, so he had time. He made a hasty decision to bury it in the backyard, just for a little while. After all, his wife was a reasonable woman. He was sure he would have received her blessing if he had explained what a great deal it was, how they were sold out in every other store, and how his friend Jacob had the old version of the game. He still could not believe it had been in stock.

He grabbed the shovel and dug a small, shallow pit. It was just big enough to hold his purchase, which he had carefully wrapped in plastic shopping bags. He covered it with dirt and placed leaves around the area to camouflage the impromptu construction zone.

He had barely enough time to wash and dry his hands before his wife pulled into the driveway. That was close! But his secret was safe, buried beneath three inches of topsoil. His house-wide reputation for being a good husband remained intact.

The very next day, as he walked home from work, he was thinking about how to introduce the item so that it would appear to have always been there. He could wait until after Christmas and let it blend in with his gifts. He could dig it up and inform her that he had bought it. No. Bad idea. He could do something to earn a few extra bucks so his purchase would seem more justified. Right about then, he walked past the store window. The clerk inside had just completed the new display, and there it sat, illuminated by sunlight and surrounded by its cheaper retail competitors. Jared's eyes glazed over and remained transfixed on the manufactured mechanism of bliss. Yeow! That was a steep price. But it was the only one he'd seen in town. Obviously, there had to be a luxury charge added because of its scarcity. If he had this, his buddy Jacob would be so jealous. Right then, a well-dressed gentleman in a suit moved beside him. He followed the man's eyes and saw they were also admiring the display. Without thinking, he moved toward the entrance to beat the other man to the register. But no. He didn't have the cash, and a credit card transaction would leave a trail. His head swiveled as he looked around hopefully for some errant $100 bills tumbling down the roadway. Perhaps a lazy armored car driver forgot to close the doors? Nope, no such luck. But wait! There was an ATM machine across the street. It would only show a withdrawal and not indicate where the purchase was made. He scurried across the street like a nut-starved squirrel. He looked over his shoulder every few seconds to make sure the other man had not gone inside. He furiously inserted his card and pressed buttons while keeping his eye on the trophy. *Hurry. Hurry! Just give me the money.* Relief flooded his heart as the green bills slid horizontally out of the slot. Jared snatched them up and re-crossed the street with a bizarre speed-walker gait. The other man was now moving toward the shop door, so he sped up to a jog and then a brief sprint.

The collision was soft, but he smiled and said, "Excuse me," as he squeezed by to enter the store.

As he walked home, he hugged the bag against his chest. There would be no money trail, but how would he explain this? It was fairly big and would draw anyone's attention. He was glad he had beaten the other man to the register, but now he needed time. He needed to hide it from his wife and devise a plan to surreptitiously introduce his great find. The shovel was waiting right where he'd left it.

They say squirrels dig so many holes in the fall that they forget where some are in the winter. This would not be his mistake. He dug up his previous quarry and reburied the items beside each other. A few scattered leaves and "voila."

The next day, he took the car because his wife was spending time with her mom. As expected, the tank was nearing empty, so he pulled into a gas station to fill up. As the numbers on the pump climbed higher with no sign of stopping, Jared considered how many tankfuls he could buy with what he had paid for his recent purchase. Two? Three? If only he had a way to save gas, he could use the savings to buy things he wanted and not just the things he needed. He contemplated various options as he drove to work when one suddenly presented itself. A man stood beside a motorcycle parked in a yard near the curb. Wow! That bike was a thing of beauty, its voluptuous fenders trimmed with pieces of shiny chrome. And that engine! He could see himself dressed in leather and revving it while waiting for the red light to change. And then the man put a "For Sale" sign on the handlebars. This was it! He could free up the car for his wife and save gas! It was pure genius.

The man graciously told him about the motorcycle and let Jared sit on it. With the turn of a key and press of a button, the big V-Twin engine roared to life, causing birds from a nearby tree to take flight.

He turned to the man and said enthusiastically, "I'll take it!"

Since Jared himself had no riding experience, the man was kind enough to drive it to his house in exchange for a ride home. That afternoon, as he waited for his wife to get home, he tried to imagine her reaction when she saw it. He tried to pretend that she would think it was cool or sexy or somehow practical, but experience told him that those were all fantasies. If only she was more interested in his wants or, make that, his needs, she could be a part of these decisions. After all, it's not entirely his fault that he hides things from her. Now, where did he put that shovel?

The hole was easily enlarged to fit the new purchase. This weekend, while Jared and his wife were doing something fun and had time to think, he would reveal the bike. She might enjoy a ride. But, no. She had mentioned several times that they would get a boat to take out on the weekends if they ever had any extra money. She wanted somewhere to lie out and work on her tan. That's it! If she had a boat, she couldn't make him feel guilty about his bike. He went inside to search the computer for nearby deals.

Thankfully, just a few miles away was a great deal. It

needed a little work after sitting out in the elements, but it was mostly cosmetic. The guy assured him that "it ran like a top" the last time he had it out.

On the way home, Jared carefully watched his rear-view mirrors as pine straw and leaves blew out of the hull. How long had it been since this boat had been in the water? He tried to remain optimistic, but the faded color and antiquated motor caused an empty pang to fill his stomach. This had been a rash and hasty decision. But it was her fault! If she had anything negative to say, it would be her being ungrateful. He was in the right. He was innocent. In the driveway, he exited his car to appraise their new vessel realistically. He may need time to clean it up before the big presentation. He needed the shovel.

The hole seemed to grow by itself with each new addition. The excess dirt became a bigger issue each time and more challenging to hide. The suspicious pile of leaves in the middle of their backyard was assuming the shape of a large hump. Time and transactions had caused him to forget exactly what was buried at the bottom of the pile. Whatever it was, he knew it had been an excellent deal and that it was essential to him. What all was buried in the pit? As he completed the latest deposit, he looked at the shovel. It was disproportionately small compared to the task that it was required to perform. Seeing that it was essential to keeping the household peace and protecting his wife, it was a critical and essential piece of equipment. An upgrade was definitely in order. Tomorrow, he would bury his old shovel with a new one.

26. THE PROGNOSIS

Our little examination room was what you'd expect. A wide strip of paper protected the padded table. The stainless-steel table on wheels displayed an ear-light, some long cotton swabs, and a small bottle of iodine. Some unimpressive and generic art was on the wall, presumably making the space more inviting. I felt silly and exposed sitting there with my legs hanging off the end of the table like a little kid. My mind wondered. *If the building caught fire, would I have a better chance of escaping if I ditched this paper gown?* The mental image was both hilarious and horrifying.

The doctor's entrance was predictable: two quick knocks followed by the activation of the door handle. He was wearing the expected white lab coat and stethoscope. In his hand was a clipboard-type chart, which engaged his full attention. He flipped through a sheet before meeting my eyes and extending his hand to shake mine. He was friendly and professional. His demeanor indicated, "I really care, but I think we both realize that there are boundaries between us."

I was feeling fine today, albeit just a tad anxious. You hear stories about people who go for a routine check-up and leave with a fatal diagnosis. It could happen...but chances are it would not.

"How are you feeling today?" The doctor greeted me.

"Fine, doc. Is everything alright?"

"Well, you're in the right place...but we need to discuss something."

Uh oh. No small talk. No pleasantries. Straight to the point. This was bad. My stomach flipped and twisted into a knot. This has the potential to be serious. This could be one of those moments where everything suddenly changes. Priorities are immediately rearranged, and the list of things that were previously so important now takes a back seat.

"Is something wrong? Did something show up?"

He pursed his lips and paused, obviously deciding how to break the news.

"Just give it to me straight, doc. I need to know."

"It's your heart."

I knew it. My grandfather had died in his 60s of a heart attack. My dad had always had high cholesterol. I silently cursed my genes.

"The official diagnosis is Hypertrophic Cardiomyopathy, but we'll just call it what it is. It's a hardening of the heart."

My mind pictured my heart turning to stone like cured concrete. I imagined great quantities of blood going in but just a trickle pumping out as the walls lost their elasticity.

"This is crazy! I don't believe it. I take good care of myself. I buy the 'heart-healthy' cereal. I don't smoke. I walk my dogs every day!" My excited state conveyed my fear. It was embarrassing, but this event superseded everyday etiquette.

My mind raced to discover an explanation, a remedy, or someone to blame.

"I don't believe you." I continued. "I feel just fine. I do the same things that everyone else does. More, actually. I eat better.

I'm more active. I take these little pills full of powdered fruits and vegetables. Heart problems are for the obese and the alcoholics and the smokers."

"Unfortunately, none of us are immune. We develop this malady partly from hereditary factors and partly from our environment."

"Like secondhand smoke? Then it's my co-worker, Jim. He smokes outside during our breaks. I'll tell him that his actions are harmful to me and that we can't hang out anymore. Problem solved."

"It's not just Jim. It's everywhere. It's in the atmosphere. Some people are just more susceptible than others."

"Then it's my grandfather's fault. He passed on heart disease to my father, and my father passed it on to me."

"Look. No one is completely healthy. If we lived in a world where perfect, disease-free children were a requirement, no one could ethically reproduce."

"Well, it's a stupid system then. Why would anyone reproduce knowing that it will result in suffering?"

"That's a fair point. But would you define your whole existence as suffering?"

I thought about it. I thought about all the things that I care about and why. I thought about how comforting my wife's embrace is. I thought about the warm sensation when my little girl crawls into my lap and puts her head on my chest. I thought about our trip to the Grand Canyon this spring. I thought about donuts.

"No. I don't really suffer."

"I'm sorry to have been the bearer of bad news. It's my least favorite part of this profession."

"You can't just have bad news. There has to be some good news, right? You can't just waltz in here, tell me I'm a goner, and then leave."

"Well, you're right that this is bad news. The heart lacks the regenerative qualities that other parts of the body enjoy. Once it is damaged, the options for care become very limited. But there is hope."

My eyes widened, and he had my full, undivided attention. It seemed like he was waiting only to build suspense.

"I know a guy." He paused again while looking left and right. This suddenly felt like a clandestine exchange of contraband.

"You know a guy? What about him? Is he an organ donor?"

"No. Not really. And I really shouldn't be mentioning him to you because it's a conflict of interest."

"How? Aren't you in the business of helping people?"

"Yes, but my options are limited. My office can offer things that combat the symptoms, provide temporary relief, or prolong the inevitable. His methods are a little outside the box."

"Then why are you telling me? Shouldn't you just write me a script and tell me to call you in the morning?"

He grinned just a little. "Good one. No, actually, this man helped me. A few years ago, I received the same diagnosis as you. This condition is more common than you'd think. I tried everything that my practice had to offer. I pulled favors, called colleagues, and tried experimental protocols. Nothing helped. Then a friend told me about this man. I was desperate. Everything I'd worked for was slipping through my fingers."

"So how does he help? Is it something holistic? Some weird tribal voodoo?"

Another grin from the doctor and a soft chuckle. "No. You actually follow him."

"Follow him?" My expression twisted into cynical confusion.

"I know it sounds trite and impossibly ineffective, but it worked for me. I followed him. I listened to him. I followed his prescription for life as best as I could. It wasn't perfect, but I couldn't deny the results. I could feel my heart getting better.

More accurately, I could finally recognize the effects of the disease as they began to dissipate. I hadn't known how bad off I was until I started to get better."

I couldn't believe he was telling me this. Firstly, because it sounded like lunacy. Secondly, because it flew in the face of modern therapies. Did I trust his advice? Who should I commit my future to? One thing is for certain. I do not want my heart to be hardened.

"I'd like to meet him."

27. The Rope

The first time I saw it, I thought it was silly. I was walking back to my office after having coffee with a client. As I cut through the park, my mind was occupied with thoughts of our future business together and what that could mean for my career. The increased revenue for our firm would probably mean a promotion for me. Maybe a new condo? Maybe a luxury car? Wait, what would I do with a car? Everything in the city is just a short walk or cab ride away.

I was so engrossed with my thoughts that I almost bumped into it. It appeared in my vision so suddenly that I ducked like Laila Ali, avoiding a haymaker. I turned to look at the peculiar protrusion. Was protrusion the right word? No. It was more like an intrusion—an intrusion on my train of thought, my way back to the office and my life. I looked at it up and down, sneered, and then turned back toward my office. It was worthless.

That afternoon spent at my desk was productive. With the new deal almost finalized, I was securing resources, establishing a new network, and sneaking the occasional peek at the BMW website. Where would I even park it? I was on fire. I was truly in the prime of life and just hitting my stride. Since wealth and success are infinite, the world seemed like my toy store.

But something behind me was vying for my attention. It was like a scratchy collar or when someone's tickling your ear with a feather to watch you slap yourself repeatedly. It was an interference on my focus, and it was irritating. The rope.

I spun in my leather chair and peered out the window. There it was, just where it had been on my way back to work. Needlessly in the way. Annoying everyone who passed by. Difficult to ignore. But ropes serve a purpose, and they can be very useful. *I do not have time to devote thought to this.*

It was difficult to celebrate that night. We clinked glasses. We drank. We smiled and made snide remarks about our competitors. But my smile was forced. I was bothered and felt unreasonably vindictive toward the rope. Why did it have to be there? Why did it have to be the fly in the ointment of an otherwise incredible day?

The next day, I was dressed for success. At least, that's what Vogue had called it. I wore my most expensive suit and shoes. I even wore makeup. A winner dresses like a winner. From now on, I would not settle for less than the best. The walk through the park was not the most efficient path to work, but maybe I was looking for a fight. Maybe I wanted to gloat to the rope and let it know that I was doing just fine without it. As I turned the corner of the sidewalk, there it was. It was almost two inches thick and about three feet off the ground. Following it upward, it passed beyond the treetops and the skyscrapers and disappeared into the clouds. Its endlessness disgusted me. But not today—today, I would win. I clenched my fists as I quickened my pace.

I walked straight to it and stopped with my face just inches away. The tendons in my neck were showing, and my lips were in a smirk. I suppose my arms of intimidation were flared out from some primordial effort to look bigger than my opponent.

"You have no right to ruin my success." My words were cold and sincere and sounded stupid in my ears. I hope no one heard me talking to a rope. "I know what you're doing. Oh, I 'get' your message loud and clear. But it's dumb. The ground isn't going anywhere. This world isn't going anywhere. It's here to stay. I'm here to stay." My anger was satisfying. It was venomous and rancid. It was sure to offend. And yet, the rope just hung there. Its silence had the effect of mocking me, and yet it wasn't. The longer it stayed there, undeterred, seemingly indifferent to my anger, the angrier I got. I slapped it. It flopped mopishly to one side. I slapped it again, but its response was lethargic. I punched it. I choked it. In my fury, I kicked at it and even tried to bear-hug it. But it showed no response whatsoever. Its condition remained utterly neutral. I was now panting. With my partially opened mouth and red face, I formulated another attack. I would pull it down. I jumped off the ground as high as I could and grabbed it firmly with both hands. When it held my weight, I was both surprised and disappointed. I looked up and saw it disappearing into partly cloudy skies above, but I could not see its terminus. I bounced and jerked down as hard as I could, but it would not budge. It didn't stretch. It didn't do anything. It just hung there with me hanging on it.

Realizing that my battering of this bewitching binding had drawn an audience, I let go and dropped to the ground. Standing in the small circle of frightened onlookers, I straightened my blouse and pulled down my suit jacket before sauntering to my office building. It was too early to admit defeat.

The day was full of emails and phone calls, some necessary and others congratulatory. I tried to sound excited and grateful, but I knew the rope was still there. It appeared out of the corner of my eye and dropped into my thoughts so often that I closed the blinds. But the cords that held them in place reminded me of my tormentor. That infuriating rope.

The feud lasted for days and even weeks. My confident and triumphant veneer became harder and harder to maintain. It exhausted me.

One night, as I tried to go to sleep, I came to the realization that I would have to deal with this once and for all. And it could not wait until morning. My sudden desire to be rid of this anguish overrode my sense of fashion. So, in gray sweatpants and my old, comfy hoodie, I left my apartment in the middle of the night to confront my nemesis.

The park was quiet and deserted when I entered. That was good. The situation could get ugly again. But I wasn't angry this time. I was curious. I wanted answers. If something so frivolous and pointless could hold this level of sway over someone of my stature, it may require further investigation. It casually held its ground as I approached.

"It's me again." I looked around to make sure we were alone. "Look. I, uh, I've been thinking. I'm pretty sure I know why you're here, and it makes me very uncomfortable." I looked around again. Still no one. "I just have a hard time believing that the world could just fall away. But still, I somehow think it could." It felt good to admit it. Honesty. There had been a longstanding cold war between my ego and my reason. The stalemate had to end. My mouth opened to speak, but the words got caught in my throat. I was at a loss for words. Me—a pro in the conference room: Ms. Verbal Judo. But here, in the silence of the park, I welcomed the relief. It seemed that the source of my frustration was also my cure. With nothing else to say that it had not heard before, I leaned my head against it. I then slid my right hand around it and pulled it close to my face. Then, my left hand. I shut my eyes and let its calming sensation wash through me. The car, the condo, the cash—they did not matter to me anymore. I was so relieved. I had never realized how much stress those goals had added to my life. But now, now I had something to hold onto. Something that was not going anywhere. Something that would hold me even if the world fell away.

The next day was humiliating. At first, the homeless and the winos made their rounds. They looked at me as if I was one of them, which was degrading. Then, the joggers passed by, pretending not to see me. Worst of all were my co-workers. They laughed, made jokes, and tried to convince me to let go and come inside. They offered to loan me a dress or even buy me one. They could not understand why I was standing there holding on to the rope we'd all been ridiculing around the water cooler. My boss even came by, showing sincere concern. He had a corporate counselor who explained (in a very patronizing tone) that prolonged stress can cause peculiar reactions and that I would be OK.

When I answered, "But I want something to hold onto when the world falls away," alarm creased their faces. Apparently, I had officially crossed over into Crazy Town.

Over the next few days and weeks, I saw someone else occupy my office on the fifth floor. This woman even exchanged jokes with my old co-workers as they walked past me to go to lunch. And yet, I hung there, both hands around the rope, my feet still on the ground. I was now an object of ridicule and scorn.

One day, a passerby saw me and moved my way to start a conversation. "A rope holder, huh? This is quite intriguing. I assume you're doing this because you are afraid."

This was my first confrontation with a stranger. "I was afraid. The world could fall away. It WILL fall away one day, and I want to be holding onto this rope when it does."

He had a studious appearance and formed his words carefully. "Might I suggest an alternative?"

I hadn't considered any alternatives. Certainly, there were drawbacks to holding this rope. "I'm listening."

"Come with me. Let's focus on the things we can control and strengthen them. You seem like a smart young woman. I'm sure we could find you an amazing position in a local firm. You could make enough money to provide whatever security you require. A strong house? A fortress even. Maybe a bodyguard."

I responded, "I've made and had money. It only added things to the list of what I could lose. And besides, the rope is free."

He considered this and changed his tack. "I see. Well, how about your health? We could visit the gym and strengthen the ol' ticker. You could live to see 90 or even 100!"

"And then what? I would certainly be needing the rope at 100! And what if I do all that exercise and get hit by a bus?"

"You are a hard one. I've convinced many to let go with less prodding. Well, what about sedation? They make pills that can ease your troubled mind. If not pills, then how about the bottle or both?"

"I felt true peace when I grabbed hold of this rope. To pursue another option would require letting go of this one."

"Well, how about this. Let go of the rope and see if anything happens. I assure you that nothing will, and you can step one foot away. Nothing will happen again, and you can step further away. The rope will remain here and wait for you if you decide to need it in the future."

"But what if it happens when I'm away from the rope? Not everyone has a warning of when their world falls away."

He studied me with hostility in his eyes. He could not immediately think of another argument. I twisted my hand so the rope was firmly wrapped around it. The act declared my final position on the matter.

"And why does my holding onto the rope bother you so? I doubt it has any effect on you whatsoever. The rope angered me, too, when it first interrupted my thoughts and ruined my false peace. Perhaps you are where I was. You are welcome to hold the rope and see if it has the same allaying effect it had on me."

And with that, he huffed, frowned, and spun to walk away angrily. I remained there, peacefully defiant, touching the ground yet tethered to the heavens.

28. THE SHACK

After nine long months at sea, it finally came into view last night. It was just before sundown, and I had the helm. At first, I thought it was a dark cloud on the horizon like the thousands of others I had scanned hopelessly. But this one did not move. And as we sailed closer, its edges crystalized. I quickly woke the crew and called for the spyglass. It was land! We celebrated with yelps and backslaps. We were going to be delivered. As the last rays of sunlight turned the tip of the island's summit to burnt orange, I oriented myself to the setting sun. Its reverse azimuth would be my guide until the stars appeared.

Sleep was restless that night for all. Would the island still be there at morning light? Although it was completely veiled in the cloak of night, we held our course and relied on the shared image our eyes had captured.

In less than eight hours, the sun completed its visit with those on the other side of the world. Then, it returned like a loyal postman. Today, however, the sun was obstructed by a lush, ungainly protrusion from the ocean. Most of the edges of the island were highlighted with nearly white sand, which contrasted nicely with the crashing blue waters of its coast. Immediately beyond was the thick carpet of palm trees and undergrowth. *What mysteries lie within?* I wondered. But the most intriguing feature was a rock spire that jutted precariously near the northern coast. It looked scalable, possibly. At its top was an almost perfectly flat plateau as if a giant samurai had sliced off the top with his sword. It was the high point and promised a commanding view of the land and sea. It appealed to me strongly and, as I would find out later, exclusively.

We rejoiced as our bow slid onto the sand and ground to a halt. Our little vessel had endured the voyage and remained intact through every wave and storm. Its sail showed evidence of wear and repair but could now rest in irons. The most appreciated aspect of our arrival was the firm ground beneath our feet. No more of the tossing and rocking, which silently exhaust the body, requiring a constant, subconscious balancing act.

We hopped off the boat and took little time to admire the beauty of our bay. We silently agreed that our arrival merited a momentary interlude. Like most humans, we were restless and curious. Truth be told, we were also selfish. Each man wanted to find and claim the best spot for his abode. After all, the primary use of this terrain would be to support a shelter. We each wandered off in the direction that seemed best to us. A silent competition ensued.

Our island offered myriad benefits and amenities. As I crested each knoll, I would discover a cascading stream or crystal-clear spring. Languid trees loomed over the water, moss from their limbs sipping its surface. But each pleasant vista was followed by disappointment, as a fellow crewman would be working nearby, having beaten me there. With a new sense of urgency, I picked up my pace and attempted to veer away from the others.

My heart began to register panic as, one by one, all of the pleasant spots were taken. Their new tenants were affable toward me and yet adamant that I should be moving on. It seemed like I had circled the whole island without finding a place to make my home. So, I stood on the beach catching my breath, my arms hanging loosely by my sides. What to do? The weather was pleasant now, but what about the changing seasons? Severe conditions would surely come. I became aware that I was standing in a shadow, a rather large shadow. I raised my eyes to find the source of this shade, and they took in the imposing monolith. It was the rocky spire that I had first noticed and been drawn to. But no, going up there was crazy. The prospect of living up there was madness. To do so would require separating from the others. It would require hard work and dangerous working conditions.

On the other hand, what choice did I have? Our little boat had been dismantled to be used as building material. I could not go back to that which was once a source of safety. My so-called friends had taken what they wanted and pushed me out. And so, I began the long, arduous climb.

The actual height of any point is only realized once you are looking down from its summit. The ensuing climb would yield a full perspective. I set my sights on the narrow path that had probably been a trail for game (most likely mountain goats). I finally plateaued at the summit and was relieved to see that there was a fair amount of greenery up here. Apparently, the rocky pockmarked surface caught and stored rainwater efficiently. Although small in dimension, the whole top was surprisingly fertile. Yes, this would do quite nicely.

For days, I lumbered up and down the steep slope to procure driftwood and whatever materials I could glean without trespassing against my mates. In my heart, I often struggled with feelings of jealousy towards my crewmates who could simply reach down to the ground to find what they needed. No perilous transport was necessary. Slowly, my shelter began to take shape; it was smaller than those of my peers due to the difficult logistics. My little mesa also afforded me a great deal of privacy. Although questions were asked and jokes were made, no one's curiosity was worth the steep ascent to my little nest.

As the summer continued, we all made improvements to our homes. Ambition and the need for progress ran through our veins. Well, it did in most of us. A few had merely set up hammocks and lean-tos. "Why bother?" they would remark. "We live in a paradise. I have the stars for a ceiling and no need for walls." Their days of slumber seemed to snicker at our efforts.

Others had sensed a need to fortify their positions. One man had exerted great effort to haul rocks from the bay back to his settlement. He dug a foundation in the sand and filled it with gravel. One by one, he set the rocks in the outline of a fortress and found clay to fill in the gaps. I could see the work clearly from my perch and was quite impressed by his progress. Another had dug deep holes in the earth into which he then sank long poles hewn from trees. He lashed other poles high upon these so that a treehouse of sorts began to take shape. This project, too, was easily surveyed from my position.

I went about securing food and offering help to others. I felt content with my dwelling and my belongings. After all, not much else would fit on my perch.

One morning, I awoke to an unusual sensation. It was cool. I sat upright and looked out of the little window I had made. Unlike every other morning, when the sky had been a pleasant blue, it was now gray and menacing. Clouds moved toward our island from some dark source on the horizon. My heart pounded audibly, and my stomach felt slightly nauseous. I watched the weather from my high lookout and wondered what the other men's reactions would be. Had they even noticed?

Just before noon, my concern got the better of me. I made my way down the slope and visited the Citadel, which is the name I had given to the rock fortress. I yelled the man's name, and he looked down over the edge at me.

"Have you noticed the weather? I think that a storm is brewing."

The man sipped from a cup and looked out apathetically at the jungle canopy. "Looks fine to me."

"But you can't see it from here. If you come up to my position, you will see that there is cause for concern."

"Concern for what? I live in a fortress. Unlike you and the others, I used my time well."

I looked again at his home, trying to find a weakness. Visually, it was impressive. But then I looked at the ground. That was it!

"But your foundation! You have built on the sand. The sea could easily wash this away, for you are on low ground."

The man's face frowned. He was obviously displeased at my evaluation and confident of his handiwork. With a belittling tone, he shouted, "Run along to your nest, little birdie, and I will stay in my castle." And with that, he disappeared behind the rampart.

It stung to be dismissed, but I quickly departed to warn the owner of the treehouse. He, too, took offense and made a great display of testing the strength of his structure. He grabbed the vertical poles and shook them with all of his might. It barely swayed. "Let the waters come! I am elevated. I have chosen a higher path." As he too refused my warning, the prideful part of me thought, *but not as high as mine.*

I visited each of my crewmen, offering the same forecast. Some showed interest. Others would not lift their woven palm hats from their faces as they rocked serenely in their hammocks. The owner of a lean-to, however, actually seemed quite alarmed by my news. He followed me to the beach and looked across the now choppy sea. "But what can I do?"

"Come with me. There is room on the rock for you."

He looked upward and lamented, "But it looks more dangerous than down here. I would be giving up trees and water and food."

"I have those things and the benefit of high ground. Please come with me."

He looked again and then back to the jungle. Indecision can be deadly. "I just don't know. I think I will go back to my shelter. Maybe the storm will pass by."

"My friend, it may be too late if you don't come now."

He looked again at the rock and back toward his shelter, his face a wavering grimace.

I offered once more, "I have offered refuge to everyone on the island, and you are the only one who has considered my advice. But I have to leave now if I want to save myself." And with that, I turned and ran toward my pillar. As I reached its base, a gust of wind flung me off course so that I faltered. But repetition had bred familiarity within my limbs. I easily climbed the little trail despite the worsening conditions. Within minutes, I was tucked away in my little shelter nestled amongst the low trees. The wind howled as the rain began to roll off of my roof.

I lay there thinking about my crewmates, wondering how they were faring below. Feelings of concern mingled with a dark desire for vindication. I did my best to fight off the latter. As the winds surged and abated, I thought I heard a voice in one of the lulls. I removed the panel from my little window and craned my head to listen more closely. Yes! There it was again. Someone was calling my name. The voice had a desperate tone. I flung open my door and moved toward the edge to see who was calling. Down at the bottom was the owner of the lean-to. He waved to me with empty hands. Apparently, nothing had been worth taking. I waved back to acknowledge him and tried to shout directions to my little path. But the storm and his unfamiliarity with this rock prevented him from finding it, although he searched frantically. *I must show him the way,* was my only thought. I moved swiftly down the muddy trail, sliding and falling often. Gravity pulled me downward as I moved further away from my security. I reached the man, who was now in a state of panic. "Follow me!" I shouted as I grabbed his arm. Together, we struggled up the incline. Growing rivulets of water washed mud past our feet. With gasping lungs, we left the low ground behind and finally reached the shelter. I shut the door and asked my new friend, "Where are the others?" He looked down and shrugged his shoulders helplessly.

All night long, the storm attacked the island. We felt the percussion of enormous waves pounding the land. Trees cracked loudly, and the rearranging of the earth could be heard. However, despite some harmless noise, it had little effect on us, which we soon grew accustomed to.

The next morning, we awoke to the familiar warmth of sunlight and clear, blue skies. We exited our shelter to survey the damage, hoping to see our friends below. There was nothing. Where the Citadel once stood was now a river where the storm surge was draining back into the ocean. Over at the treehouse, broken poles were the only remains of the structure. Elsewhere, the jungle had been washed clean of any evidence that we had ever landed here. The wall of water had erased our efforts effortlessly.

29. The Slide

I don't remember ever getting on the slide. I was just on it. It wasn't steep at all, almost level, which is good because I was so very small when I became cognizant. The decline was so imperceptible that I had to exert great effort to scoot even an inch! But the billboards—those magnificent, intriguing, beguiling billboards. They were posted on both sides at ever-increasing frequency. Even before I could read, they were promoting and offering their fares insistently.

The first ones exhibited attention. They certainly caught my attention, and I wanted theirs. First, my mother's, then my father's. Then, anyone's including relatives, friends, and strangers. Whatever the situation, I wanted it to be about me. The next billboards displayed a huge variety of toys. Some appealed to me more than others, but the ones I desired most were the ones others were playing with.

Further billboards varied in size depending on what foods they were advertising. The ones displaying vegetables were very small and hidden in the shadows of massive marketing marquees, which, illuminated with bright spotlights, showed desserts, sweets, candies, cakes, sodas, milkshakes, and anything with sugar. I was instantly hooked.

All this time, my slow ride down the slide required great effort. I would dig my heels into the smooth surface as best as I could and pull my bottom with my feet. I would try to help with my hands and arms, but I found almost no purchase on the rounded sides. But my yearning gave me strength and determination. Each billboard captured my thoughts and became my sole focus until the next one appeared. I pursued each offering one by one, obviously preferring some over others.

It seems that my parents had some existing vendetta against some of the marketing firms. With great effort, I would see them purposefully obscuring some of the advertisements. They would pluck up the smaller, less desirable signs and wave them frantically in front of some of the larger ones. Sometimes they were successful, and sometimes they were not.

With time, moving down the slide required less effort, in part because I was getting stronger and more proficient. The second factor was one I did not immediately realize. Three decades later, I realized that a factor of physics was acting upon me and assisting me on my journey. The slide was getting steeper.

I actually enjoyed the increase in momentum. Velocity was exciting. I was finally going places. Chasing me down the slide had become quite taxing for my parents, and they eventually gave up the pursuit. They wished me well and did their best to communicate their affection as my increasing speed continued to pull me away.

The billboards had somehow optimized their exposure so that my favorites were now positioned directly beside the slide and so large in size that the smaller, less popular offerings almost vanished. The balance of those days brought me great pleasure. I was able to obtain the objects of my desire with considerably less effort than when I was younger. As I continued to pick up speed, I assumed that my ability to consume and experience pleasure would also increase.

About four decades into my ride, a peculiar awareness began to creep into the corners of my mind. The billboards had become spectacular. They were now positioned directly overhead, and their offerings were available to me in an instant. And yet, they no longer elicited the same feelings of eager desire. I felt quite bored and looked behind me at the avalanche of accumulated objects that now followed me down the slide. Any bend or bump in the slide could result in a catastrophe for me. It was also at this time that the steepness of the slide became very apparent. I began to force the soles of my shoes against the slick surface and push my palms outwards to slow my momentum, but my efforts yielded minimal results.

At that time, I also looked back at my freight train of merchandise and noticed the back of the billboards. Unbeknownst to me, there was information printed there about the side effects of each product. The billboard advertising turkey said, "May cause sudden sleepiness. Have nap time pre-scheduled." The warnings on the back of the beer billboard read, "May cause a large stomach paunch over time. May alter your standards for women. May cause behavior that you will regret." The words on the back of the car billboards warned, "Don't forget about your insurance coverage, regular maintenance, regular washing and vacuuming, volatile gas prices, tires, repairs, scratches, dings, traffic jams, aggressive drivers, and depreciation." Wow! I'm glad I didn't see those before my last acquisition.

Six decades in, the angle of my descent was about forty-five degrees. For years, I had been looking over my shoulder to read the warnings of consequences that I already knew from experience. Hindsight truly is 20/20. I had abandoned any attempts to slow down and began to look over the arching horizon to see what lay at the bottom. An ending seemed inevitable, and I felt like I should be "assuming crash positions." I looked back at the mountain of merchandise that tumbled and slid behind me. Perhaps I should begin to toss some of the items over the rail to lessen their inevitable impact on me. And what exactly happens at the bottom? How steep would the slide get? Would I eventually be in free fall, helpless to direct myself in any capacity?

Perhaps it was desperation, but I discovered a way to alleviate the dread of what lay ahead. The billboards had begun to mock me, offering solutions that had long since ceased providing relief, adding to my downward momentum. It took a concerted effort, but I closed my eyes tightly and let them pass unnoticed. Even with my eyes shut, I could feel their presence passing all around me. But, with time, they retreated from the edges of my slide and seemed to have decreased in size. In an effort to "come clean," carefully worded variations of their warnings were now displayed in fine print below their offerings on the front of the billboards. But no matter, I had developed the ability to ignore them, and they responded in kind.

At that time, I also began to unload, piece by piece, the cargo which had accompanied me for so long. As each item tumbled over the edge and into oblivion, I wished it well, hoping it might provide someone else more use or pleasure than I had received. Ultimately, there were still some items, both essential and non-essential, that followed me downward, but it was acceptable by my new standards.

Now, seventy years into my decline, I contemplated how best to meet my end. I had reduced the cumbersome collateral, but something about my orientation still seemed misaligned. It happened by accident that I suddenly found myself rotated one hundred and eighty degrees. A sudden curve in the slide had spun me around so that my head was now leading, with my feet behind. Although I now had a much clearer perception of my speed and destination, I also recognized that this position afforded some previously unrecognized (or unneeded) benefits. I no longer feared the onslaught of what followed me down the slide. The termination of my tour would not come as much of a surprise. I also found that extending my arms above my head made the ride much smoother. With great surrender and no distractions, I finally and successfully concluded my ride down the slide.

30. The Solution

"Wunderbar! I've done it!" crowed Professor Kimmelkopf.

The German-accented announcement permeated the small laboratory. The stainless-steel tables covered with beakers, test tubes, and scientific instruments sat unmoved and unimpressed. But Kimmelkopf's faithful assistant, Siegfried, drew near with genuine curiosity to see what his mentor had accomplished.

The tall, gray-headed scientist stood holding a glass container at about eye level. He gazed at the perfectly clear liquid held within and smiled contentedly. The spotless lab coat he wore had no wrinkles whatsoever. It was a mark of the excellence that guided his life's work and everyday decisions.

"What is it?" Siegfried meekly inquired. He was almost a foot shorter than his teacher, and his stooped posture and averted expressions exacerbated the difference.

Kimmelkopf continued to stare at the elixir. "This," he paused, "is the ultimate solution. It has the power to dissolve any and all impurities. So much so that it will purify any liquid it comes into contact with." He turned the beaker as he triumphantly examined it for discolorations he knew would not be there. "The applications are limitless."

Siegfried smiled supportively and naively asked, "Like what?"

The taller scientist broke his gaze away from the container and looked downward at his portly protégé. "Like what?" His expression was now stern and incredulous. "Just think of it! Theoretically, you could pour a cup of this into a pool of sewage, and it would become clear liquid. You could spray this on graffiti, which would then disappear like magic! You could remove any stain, take away any odor, and clean up any crime scene. And the medical benefits! The most microscopic dose could replace chemotherapy! Antibodies would become obsolete. The pharmaceutical industry would go bankrupt!"

Siegfried looked confused as he often did. "But why a microscopic dose? Is it expensive to produce?"

Kimmelkopf tilted his head from side to side as he answered. "Well, yes and no, but that is not the problem. It is the strength! Any more than a microgram would instantaneously convert the patient's blood into the elixir. It would overwhelm the production of the blood marrow!" His voice was almost shrill as he described the potential consequences. Siegfried seemed to cower as if reprimanded.

His teacher continued. "Quick! We must perform a test. Something crude and expedient would be appropriate."

Siegfried began to scour the tables for a suitable vessel. Of course, it would have to be sterilized and prepared for a sample. He began to unlock a nearby autoclave.

"No, no, no!" With great frustration, Kimmelkopf moved toward a trash can beside the door. With his free hand, he reached inside and removed what he was looking for. "This is perfect."

Siegfried frowned at the Styrofoam coffee cup that

Kimmelkopf had placed on the spotless work surface. It still held about 2 inches of murky coffee, some visible grounds, and a chewed piece of gum. "I need a Pasteur!"

Siegfried obeyed and returned with a sealed dropper with a small bulb on the end. The scientist removed the Pasteur from the wrapper and squeezed the bulb as the tip lowered into his new solution. With practiced slowness, he moved the dropper over the coffee cup and, with great delicacy, squeezed until a single drop fell into the sludgy beverage. The brown quickly faded to khaki and then clear. The coffee grounds became smaller by the moment until they, too, faded from sight. The gum obstinately held its ground for a few seconds more. Both sets of eyes widened at the now clean interior of the cup.

Siegfried smiled proudly. It was his master's doing, but he'd always been supportive and attentive. Besides, he drew pleasure from his teacher's abilities. This solution would change the world. No mess was its match. It was inexhaustible, self-replicating, thorough. The only thing it needed now was distribution.

31. The Storm

The arrhythmic banshee-like wail of the wind outside juxtaposed with the repetitive grinding of metal inside the small shed. The two men worked studiously, file in one hand, snow boot in the other. Their crampons needed sharpening from time to time as the snow often gave way to the rock below. That tended to dull the edges needed to bite into ice like a relentless pit bull. Not only was it a necessary act of maintenance, but it also helped pass the time on long shifts like tonight. The weather report had been wretched: plummeting temperatures, gusting winds, freezing rain, everything opposite of the protection offered by their hut. It was robustly built not only for survival but also for comfort. Its thick, rugged walls were thoroughly insulated to form a complete airtight envelope. Its seal was so precise that an air-to-air heat exchanger was included in its design to ensure the availability of fresh air.

John and Thomas noticed peripherally that the last vestiges of sunlight, which had been struggling all afternoon to penetrate the dark swirling cloud mass, were finally falling behind the ragged horizon of peaks in the distance.

"Ought to be a quiet night," John said to Thomas. "Everyone should be inside on a night like this."

Thomas paused his sharpening only long enough to glimpse the muted sunset. He nodded his agreement. Their monotonous task continued.

The evening passed with periods of busywork punctuated with patches of stilted conversation. John and Thomas had known each other and worked together for several years. The sporadic yet inevitable need for search and rescue in the national park had forged their skills as well as their character. It was the reason they stood vigil in this tiny outpost far away from civilization on such a grim and dreary night.

After completing the last item of their duty checklist, they adjusted the building's controls and prepared for bed. The radio quietly clicked and squawked with various traffic throughout the region. Their finely tuned ears had become desensitized to anything but the unique tone used to activate their services. Even indoor duty can be taxing when the weather is foul. The men ended their conversation and slipped into sleep as soon as they pulled up their wool blankets.

Good sleep is warm and womblike. Cares and concerns are veiled behind heavy eyelids. The body and mind switch modes to rejuvenate and repair. It could be an endless indulgence for the undisciplined. In the cabin, the view from a surveillance camera could be mistaken for a photograph; its stillness broken only by rising and falling chests.

Di di di di di di -Da da da da da da! The radio crowed like an insistent rooster. It was their station's tone, and their bodies responded accordingly. They quickly swung their legs out of bed and automatically began to don snowsuits and thick socks. John grabbed the microphone and pressed the transmit button.

"Alpha-Three-Tango, we received your tone and are standing by." The men continued to dress, although there did exist a faint (but hopeful) chance that this was merely information and that they would not have to go outside. Their warmed and waiting beds beckoned to their not-quite-rested bodies.

"Alpha-Three-Tango, we have a report of two missing snowmobilers. A 37-year-old white male and a 10-year-old white female are overdue. The father and daughter were reported missing by the child's mother, who lives at Valley's End. She reports that they texted just before leaving Mitchville at 10:30 p.m."

Both men visualized the likely route between the two points and mentally flipped through the various possibilities for why the snowmobilers did not reach their destination: out of gas, engine trouble, tree down, accident, white-out blizzard, hypothermia. Like most first responders, a pragmatic view of tragedy allowed them to operate calmly in the theater of chaos.

The dispatcher continued in a level (and seemingly heartless) tone. "I've advised the mother that rescue may not be possible tonight due to weather conditions. Several storm watches have been broadcast on all channels."

It was a callous but calculated reprieve that had been offered. After all, wearing the ranger's patch on their shoulders did not exclude them from the laws of nature and physics. They were susceptible to the elements just as the father and daughter were. Besides, it was probably foolish for a rescue crew to attempt the trek in these conditions. There was no reason for the father's mistake to endanger anyone else. But it had.

Thomas looked John in the eye. "So whaddaya think?"

As if to answer for them, a furious gust of chilled arctic air scratched against and rattled the exterior of their shelter. The instinct for self-preservation is as natural as the need to breathe. Our bodies and minds have built-in sensors for danger that quickly retract the hand from a hot stove or immobilize the legs in moments of indecision. To go outside would be dangerous, potentially even fatal. At best, it would be horribly uncomfortable to any warm, dry skin that was not hidden beneath Gore-Tex and insulation.

One man's answer would speak for both of them. They had always operated as one and were bound by an honor that rivaled marriage.

With grim determination in his eyes, John spoke. "I'm going."

32. THE WALK

Are we going for a walk?! A walk! Yes! We're going for a walk. My tail involuntarily wags like a windshield wiper. It honestly has a mind of its own. I bounce left and right on my paws like I'm walking on hot sand. This is *so* exciting! Somewhere in my mind, I know we did this just a few hours ago and a few hours before that, but *who cares*?! We're going for a walk!

My master puts the harness over my head and snaps the buckles. I tolerate it because I know we won't leave until I do. I've tried to show him and explain to him that it's really not necessary, but he insists.

Finally! He opens the door (because I can't do doorknobs. No thumbs.), and we are off to explore a world of endless possibilities. My nose confirms what my sensory memory already knows. We are going to discover all sorts of news and treats on this walk. Down the steps and to the right on our sidewalk. My nose leads me on this familiar trek (although we mix it up sometimes). Let's get down to business and see what's been going on; wait a second. I stop and lower my nose within an inch of a nearby fence post. My nostrils flare and fluctuate several times in one second, but it's enough. I knew it. Black Cat was here (a few more sniffs) just a few minutes ago! Doesn't he know this is my turf? How many times must I yell through our window that he is not welcome here? He or any of his cat friends. I take two steps forward and lift my right rear leg like a furry yoga instructor. Ahh. A few drops of urine ought to make my point. This area is officially dominated, protected, and governed by me—Henry. Now, we can keep going.

This neighborhood is the *best*. I've found chicken bones, old cups lined with pink-sticky sweetness, a truly fantastic stick and —what else—there was that slug. A little salty but not too bad.

My master holds the leash, and my pace keeps it barely loose. I know he means well, but I really don't need it. Maybe it's for his benefit? I've seen other masters with dark glasses and long white sticks following their guides through city streets. Their leash is more like a handle but—same difference. I love him, so I don't mind guiding my master through the neighborhood. After all, Mr. Kitty could be lurking around any corner.

My nose is taking in the news of the day. Interesting, it looks like a new neighbor moved in recently. Ahh. A few drops of urine should let him know that I already dominate, protect, and govern this block. But welcome to him anyway. Wait a second. We stop. I lower my nose. My nostrils flutter. Is that...? Yep! Definitely a raccoon (more sniffs) two, no, three of them (more sniffs). They must have been on a trash run, a quick snatch-and-grab. I've gotta hand it to them. They are the undisputed masters of scavenging. I respect that. A few drops of urine should inform them that this area is now off-limits.

Ooooh! This next block is my favorite. The leash goes tight as I pick up my pace. My nose is up in the air, and so is my tail. There it goes again. Back and forth steadily, but not frantically.

This booty is usually a sure thing. I lead my master to a small box mounted on a post. I could stand up on my rear legs to reach it, but, once again, no thumbs! A cruel handicap. But he opens the door using his thumbs (showoff) and pulls out a small, bone-shaped object. I know it's a counterfeit, but it still crunches and has a flavor, and feels so good going down into my stomach. Admittedly, my criterion for palatability is liberal. I've learned that sitting on my haunches is the most likely way of receiving this delectable, life-giving, joy-inducing sustenance. "Who's the good dog?" he asks. I've yet to answer this mystery of the universe, but he holds his open palm down near my muzzle, and I eagerly take it. I find many wonderful treats on these walks, but the best ones come from the hand of my master.

We continue and are about to cross the street. I move forward, head down, sniffing for the next bit of news or nourishment, but, Oh! The leash goes taut. I look back over my shoulder and ask my master, "Why are we stopping? There's no reason to stop." I'm pretty sure the next block is going to yield some good stuff. I try to go forward, but he is adamant. I try a few more times, but he just stands there. He does this sometimes. I don't get it.

Whooosh! A car shoots by just a few feet away. Whoa! That was close. The leash goes slack as he begins to move, and so do I.

Ahh. This is my favorite event of the day. Out for a walk with my master. It's almost as good as breakfast time, or dinner time! It's almost as good as nap time or when "Papa" comes to visit. Papa always has treats in his pocket. He doles them out (way more generously than my master). Then Papa scratches my ears and asks me that same enigmatic question. Will someone please tell me who this mysterious "good dog" is?

We take a right at the next corner, and (unbeknownst to me) volatile oils are in the air. They will enter my nose and be drawn into the mucus deposits of my nasal cavity, where sensory cells will send the data through a network of axons to the olfactory bulb in my brain. It will process the potency, age, type, source, and direction of any intoxicating scent. The processed air will be expelled through my outer nares so as not to pollute the next sample. If it was interesting, I could smell something through up to 80′ of water.

Pow! The scents hit me full force. Smelling is more than just a pastime for me. Oh no. It's much more than that. It resonates within me and can hijack my mood. Seriously. I've got what's known as a Jacobson's Organ in the nasal cavity above my mouth. It doesn't so much register scents as it does the microscopic particles in the air. Unlike my other sensory receptors, this one is hardwired to my emotions. It connects with the deepest urges and innate desires of my mind. This particular scent is not like the bone-shaped treat, not like Black Cat's infringement, not like the raccoon's looting. This is roadkill. The gamey fragrance is so strong that even my master squinches his nose in disgust. But to me, pure ecstasy. The leash goes tighter than it has all morning, but I will not be denied. All four paws are locked into "high traction" mode as I claw my way toward the mouthwatering mound of fur and flesh; it's a small squirrel that met his demise only a few hours before. I am halfway to my goal when my master's voice rings out in a loud shout. "Henry! No!" The leash goes super tight, and my front paws lift off the ground. My eyes are set on the palatable pancake near the road's center line. Nothing else matters. His voice again with a serious and softer tone. "Henry...no." My eyes are still locked on the decaying delight, but something else begins registering in my brain. Disappointment saturates my being as I start to realize that my master is not going to budge. I do not want to relent. I pull forward again, but the leash might as well be tied to an oak. I look back over my shoulder and give him my most desperate, pleading face, my brown eyes begging for empathy. But his face is serious. Our eyes are locked. I am torn. I want to obey him. I want to be like this mysterious "good dog" he keeps asking me about. But I want that filth just as badly —maybe more. In my defense, I truly cannot help it. I am wired that way.

33. The Warden

U s versus them. *Good and evil. Right and wrong. Guards and inmates.* Martin considered the bars that separated himself from the prisoner lying lazily on the cot just beyond. As he looked at the sleeping miscreant, he thought. *As expected, he is contributing absolutely nothing to society. Just sleeping and eating and costing money from the good, honest taxpayers. On the other hand, he isn't out robbing or vandalizing. So, at least he's not actively destroying the world. Perhaps a neutral is better than a negative. It's a shame he's consuming oxygen.*

And these were Martin's more munificent musings. Most of his inner contemplations relegated the inmates to something subhuman. They were the trash of the world in his mind, and this was the landfill where they had been dumped, hopefully to rot and decompose quickly.

The bars, not even two inches thick, were a physical boundary between him and this thief, drug dealer, con man, or whatever title his sins had branded him. But the actual gulf between them was miles or oceans or even worlds. He had never stolen anything, at least nothing that deserved a court appearance. He had never sold drugs. Of course, everyone experiments during high school. And he was a paragon of integrity. Sure, some of the inmates had accused him of being abusive or authoritative. But it was dangerous work, being trapped in here with all of these animals. He had to do what he had to do to stay alive.

And so, he continued his rounds. "Babysitting" is what he and the other guards had always called it. And with parental authority, they performed their duties day after day. The attitude was certainly there, even if their words didn't betray them. Any human capable of perceiving would have noticed the glint in the eye, the lip sneer, or the menacing body language that signaled hostility.

After the routine work was done, the guards settled in for another eleven hours of tedium. As he sat at the control desk with a friend, he broke the silence. "Wanna go flip some cells?"

After only a moment of contemplation, Todd replied, "Sure! Let's go find some contraband."

Although neither said it aloud, they both knew they would not be reporting everything they confiscated. Sure, they would complete the appropriate paperwork if it were something serious, like a shank or some drugs. But other, lesser discoveries need not be turned over.

The lock buzzed noisily, and Martin and Todd were instantly in a cell. The inmate rolled from his bunk and stood up, wobbling on his feet, his eyes blinking in the light. Todd held a nightstick just below his chest as Martin began to flip the mattress and strip the sheets. There was no explanation, no asking permission. They searched every inch of the cell, including the prisoner and his clothing. Martin rifled through a small stack of letters, letting them fall on the floor one by one. *Nothing good here. Just a few letters from a girlfriend. Not sure why anyone would want to date this loser.*

They left the inmate and the mess without a word. The

heavy door clanged shut behind them as they moved to another random cell. "EERRRRRRRRNNNNT!" The lock buzzed loudly as the two ambushed the cell containing their next prey. Paydirt! The prisoner's eyes widened as he frantically tried to stuff a nudie magazine under his blanket. Too late. Martin snatched it up and thumbed through a few pages as Todd tapped his nightstick on an open hand. Martin rolled up the magazine and stuffed it in his back pocket. Again, he flipped the mattress and found an assortment of forbidden items. There was a gold chain with a pendant, a few loose cigarettes, and a few dollars. *Hmmm. Probably turn in the chain and keep the rest. The chain is likely fake anyway.*

They roughly searched the prisoner and found a picture of a baby girl who appeared to be around one year old. Again, Martin unceremoniously let it fall to the ground. The prisoner followed it with his eyes crestfallen. He almost spoke but then met Todd's eye. His guard's smirk told the prisoner that it was not worth it. The two left the small room with their growing cache of goods.

The third cell was even more lucrative. Somehow, that inmate had procured a small radio with headphones. It would be perfect for listening to football games. He also had a deck of cards, a bag of candy, and some beef jerky. None of it necessarily had to be reported, so, of course, it went into the guards' own "miscellaneous" bin.

They left the third cell feeling like they'd done enough work for the time being. They split their plunder and parted ways, each aware that there were limits that they didn't need to push.

Martin was walking down a corridor, thumbing through his new magazine, when he suddenly crashed into an obstacle. The obstacle, unfortunately, was standing in the middle of the hallway. It was large and authoritative and wearing a white, starched shirt. Martin quickly recovered and hastily tried to stash away the contraband as he awkwardly addressed the "obstacle."

"Hi, Warden. Didn't expect to see you down here in the blocks." Martin's eyes darted wildly as he wished someone else could share in the spotlight. But there was no one. The warden stared at him pointedly yet wordlessly. Silence had a way of pulling a confession from a trapped suspect. "I, uh, we were just completing some cell inspections. I know how you, uh, require a few of those each shift." He shifted from foot to foot, unable to maintain eye contact for more than a moment.

"So, tell me what you think of our tenants." The warden's question seemed so out of place that Martin visibly recoiled. Was it absurd? Was it extraordinarily insightful?

"What do you mean? Are you talking about the inmates?"

"Inmates. Prisoners. Tenants. Guests. Humans. It's all semantics."

This was one of the things he could not understand or appreciate about the warden. He seemed to have an almost sympathetic disposition toward the prison population. If he had been more stern or calloused, the guards would have regarded him as more of a peer than an adversary.

"Well..." he looked down as he answered. "I guess they all deserve to be here. I guess some are worse than others." He wanted to add that most would be executed before midnight if it were up to him.

The warden inhaled and looked up as he digested this. "So how do you think you would do here, not contributing to society, devoid of privacy, subject to random searches?"

Uh oh. Martin could tell where this conversation was heading. "Sir, I don't think I will ever have to worry about that. These are criminals. These tenants, as you say, would start a riot, burn this place down, and kill us all if they had the chance."

"Tell me why many of these guys are in here to begin with."

This was exhausting. Why was the warden always asking such obvious questions? Was he slow, or did he think I was? Martin couldn't hide his exasperation. As he rolled his eyes, he exhaled. "Some of them are thieves, some of them are drug dealers, some of them are violent offenders."

The warden considered this. "I see. So, some of them took things from others and kept them. Some of them handled controlled substances like cocaine, heroin, or even tobacco. And some threatened others with a gun or, say, a nightstick."

Martin's heart began to pound. He felt sweat forming on his palms and temples. His neck felt warm. How could the warden have known? Had there been cameras in the cells? Had someone been watching him? He decided to shift gears. He whipped out the magazine and fished out the cigarettes and dollar bills. "I was just taking these to the evidence locker to report them!" He found himself shoving them into the hands of the warden. He just wanted to get rid of the evidence. Oh no! Only criminals had evidence. What was going on here?

The warden looked down at the contraband and then fixed his gaze on Martin. What was his expression? Was it sadness? Anger? Concern? More silence followed.

"I'm not what you're thinking. I'm not like them!" Martin's voice had taken on a child-like quality. "I'm not a criminal!" Anger and shame flooded his veins. He was angry at the warden, angry at the inmates, and angry at himself. Everything had conspired to put him in this position. "You tolerate way too much as it is! You wanted us to search the cells! You let things get smuggled into the prison! You trust guards who shouldn't be trusted!" This last statement hung in the air. Had he just condemned himself?

34. Theme Park

I could not go to sleep. The sole focus of my thoughts was only a twelve-hour drive away (if we didn't stop to look at any boring stuff). Yes, tomorrow morning, we will hop in the car and head south, hopefully at the crack of dawn. Perhaps we might even get there in time to ride a few rides or play a few games before the park closed at 10:00 p.m. I know that's closing time because I've read the brochure. Actually, I've memorized it. Even though I've never been there, I know where every attraction is located, and I've taken the liberty of prioritizing which ones should be ridden first. Yes, if all goes well, no flat tires or sick little brothers, we will be arriving tomorrow evening at The Wild Funtier

I know that I'm the envy of everyone in my fifth-grade class. My friend Andrea says her family is going this summer, but in a moment of parental genius, my folks planned our trip for spring break. The beauty of this is that no one can corrupt my imagination with their descriptions. Inevitably, prior knowledge of something takes away from its mystery. The Wild Funtier is the manufacturing center of dreams. At least, it had been the subject of mine every night for the last week. Perhaps that is due to my unwavering bedtime study of the brochure.

I'm not sure if I slept at all last night, but the day is finally here. Mom and Dad are checking and rechecking our luggage. I am bouncing in place. Brett says he has to pee, so that's another five-minute delay (which, by my math, is five fewer minutes riding rides). I am now pacing like a much older person. Dad wants to switch out the expired insurance card for the current one. Mom thought she saw it on the kitchen counter. My heart is pounding, I'm clinching my fists, and I could explode.

We're finally off. I'm trying to calm down.

The next ten hours are interminable. I know that's a big word, but spelling bees are my thing at school. Winning first place this year is one of the reasons we're going. I find that very remunerating (even if that's not the right word, you can be sure I've spelled it correctly). With each billboard we pass, I feel flutters of excitement in my heart. I wonder who will see the park first? We exit the interstate, and everything is themed to match the park; from the road signs to the shaped topiaries, it all reeks of The Wild Funtier.

When we pull up to the Alamo Lodge, I can't get out of the car fast enough. Every detail begs to be explored. Each employee adds to the magic with their costumes, funny accents, and jokes. *Hurry up! Just forget the luggage! We'll get it later!*

Dad insists on checking into the room. *Alright. We can drop off the bags and still get in a few hours. Hopefully, everyone is OK with skipping dinner.* My parents know we need to burn off some energy, so they grab the room key, and we head toward the Golden Spike Rail System. That's when the cell phone rang.

Dad looks at the number, frowns, and then exchanges a strange look with my mom. There was something they had not told us. She shrugs, and he reluctantly answers. With this sudden intrusion threatening to jeopardize my trip, I would gather as much intel as possible.

"Hi, Deb... Yeah, just made it... Yeah, no problems on the drive... OK... OK.. Really?... I was afraid of that... I know... I'm really sorry... No one can help the timing... OK... Thanks for calling... Give everyone our love... Bye."

I read in school that a body language researcher determined that 55% of communication was gestures, posture, and expression. 38% was the tone of voice. That meant that only 7% actually consisted of words. This came to my mind as Dad hung up the phone and had a private conversation with Mom consisting only of shrugs, head tilts, and twisted eyebrows.

"What?" I demanded. My words sounded very adult and terse to my 10-year-old ears. "What is it? What's going on?"

My heart sinks as my dad kneels on one knee to look me in the eye. The last time he'd done this was shortly before they took our dog to the vet when he'd gotten too old to walk anymore. I quickly make a mental list of tragedies that would merit interrupting our trip: famine, earthquake, nuclear blast beyond our fall-out radius. Nope—I didn't see any mushroom clouds on the horizon, so the trip should continue as planned.

"Sweetheart, that was Aunt Deb."

I know who Aunt Deb is. What? What? What!

"She said that your Great Aunt Tina has been admitted to the hospital with chest pains. The doctors aren't sure if it's a heart attack, but they're running tests. Deb and Ronny are heading over there right now."

"Great Aunt Tina? Who's that?" I really didn't know.

"It's your grandfather's aunt. She's ninety-three. You met her as a baby at the last Hadley reunion."

I feel both a huge relief and confusion. It wasn't anybody we knew, so it wasn't anyone we really cared about. Right? No big deal. Now, let's go check out the Golden Gate Games!

"Your mother and I talked about it and think that if anything happens, we should go to the funeral...to support the family."

He was so serious. The glum face and somber tone were completely unlike those of the dad I'd seen in the television commercial. That guy was delirious from all the fun.

"So, what does this mean?" I asked.

He looked again at Mom. "If we get that phone call, we may have to cut our trip short."

The news struck my heart like a dagger. Later in life, I would associate this unique and painful sensation with being dumped by a boy I liked. Emotions flooded my mind, filtered down through my neck, and permeated each limb and appendage. I suddenly hated Great Aunt Tina with a darkness that wished she was dead. Ironically, her death would signal the end of our vacation, so I had to quickly re-direct my anger. Maybe the doctors would examine her and determine it just to be a bad case of gas. The family would secretly begin to think of her as a hypochondriac, and she would feel shame for upsetting everybody. *Yeah. That would teach her.*

My dad could clearly interpret the confusion in my eyes. He tried to console me. "Look. She could be just fine. Now, let's go check out the Grand Canyon Coaster or the Seattle Skyline Swings!"

His sudden switch to enthusiasm sickens me. Maturity is not a hallmark of fifth-graders, and I decided to exhibit this deficiency shamelessly.

Tears squeeze from my squinted eyes and run down my reddened cheeks. "Why does she have to ruin everything? Why can't she leave our family alone? I won the spelling bee! We just got here! Now we can't enjoy any of it!" My bottom lip was quivering, and my chest was heaving. My mom stooped down and rubbed my back.

I whipped my shoulder back, signaling I was in no mood to

be coddled. In retrospect, the public sobbing was not in keeping with the tough-girl act. Yet, my parents were patient and gentle. They gave me a minute and spoke again.

"Sweetie." It was my mom. "I'm so sorry you heard that call. We knew it was possible, but we were hoping for better news. You have a choice to make right now. You will have to make many choices like this in years to come." Her voice then takes on a firmer tone than I was expecting. "You can be miserable, or you can make the most of this. We will probably be able to enjoy the trip just like we had planned. But there's a chance we may not. Unfortunately, life will always be uncertain. Your reaction will always be your choice."

It was the first time I remember my mom speaking to me as an adult. My tears took a few more minutes to subside, but I felt things changing within. I reasoned, and I considered options. For some reason, I thought of how much money and effort this trip had cost my parents.

Then I chose.

35. THREE MEALS

On the western edge of our town is the industrial area. Gray metal buildings trimmed with black dust line the fractured streets whose concrete curbs welcome only weeds. Filthy dump trucks belch smoke and rumble around like guard dogs, warning the cleaner, smaller vehicles to stay away.

Tucked within this dark forest of fences and asphalt is a small café. The smudged sign near the curb reads "Kim's Korean Soul Food." It's not that there is a sizeable Asian population in our town, but the owners had recognized a business opportunity decades ago when they first immigrated. No one fed the small army that worked in this district daily. After a good deal on a run-down building and a ton of hard work, Kim's now has the monopoly on lunch.

From 11:00 a.m. until 1:00 p.m., the place is packed. Walking in the front door, you feel the buzz of hustling waiters. Trays of food are being distributed to a table full of uniformed laborers or to their bosses, who looked markedly different with dress shirts and ties. The segregation is unspoken but understood and accepted. Neither group wants their world to mix with the other's.

On this particular day, a group of dapperly dressed men stood up to leave. Meanwhile, a group of men in yellow work jackets standing near the entrance eyed their table and subconsciously noted the excess of plates and glasses. Appetizers, entrees, and desserts were the norm for the management group. Not one of them requested a box for leftovers. The men laughed as they grabbed their sports coats and headed to the register. One had pulled out a stylish leather billfold to pay, but the female clerk informed him that his bill had already been paid. She nodded her head toward one of the other men. It was the vice president of a neighboring manufacturer. They had met recently to discuss possible joint ventures.

Well, that was nice of him, he thought. However, the more strategic part of his mind questioned the other man's motives. *Did he expect a $15 meal to sway my decisions? I've received way more generous incentives to do business from other partners. Am I now indebted to him? That was a jerk move—to buy my lunch so that I might feel obligated to him.* And so, the lunch and the simple act of kindness were tainted.

At another table, men were hungrily stuffing food into their mouths like livestock. Their conversation consisted more of low-brow humor, women, hunting, trucks, and beer. They weren't bad guys. They worked hard. They were often brutally honest with each other and didn't have façades. They helped each other out with no expectation of returning favors. As they stood to leave, they left a tornado zone of crumbs, dropped food, and spilled drinks. The busboy would definitely be spending some extra time here. In their defense, their plates were empty—no need for takeout boxes. A young worker reached into his back pocket for his wallet. When his hand found nothing, he let out an expletive. His mind thought back to that morning: running late, grabbing a piece of week-old birthday cake for breakfast, grabbing his keys...but not his wallet. He grimaced at his newfound position. A buddy behind him noticed as they waited in line to pay.

"Forgot your wallet." It was more of a statement than a question.

"Yeah. I was running late this morning and ran out of the house without it." Another expletive.

"I got you, man." He pulled extra bills out of his wallet to support his offer.

A worried face changed to one of relief. Kindness casts a broad net. "Thanks, man. I owe you one."

"Oh, you owe me one, alright," the other man shot back with a good-natured smile. "I still haven't forgotten about Stephanie."

The first man humorously feigned ignorance about the girl they had been vying for at the bar a few nights ago. "Man, I can't help that the ladies always go for me. You know I try to throw you my leftovers."

"Man, that cuts deep."

But the men were smiling warmly. Their constant poking and jabbing were their way of silently asking, "Do you trust me? Do you really believe I'm your friend?" You don't kid with people you don't like.

On a nearby barstool sat a lone bag lady, Bertha. Instead of a uniform, she was wearing dirty, tattered clothes. No one was doing her laundry. She ate her meal quickly but cast a furtive eye around the café. She looked uncomfortable and shifty. When the waiter asked Bertha if she needed anything else, she shook her lowered head and said nothing. Her rolled shoulders and bent body position said she did not want to be noticed. After finishing her plate and drinking the rest of her soda, she stuffed a handful of crackers into her coat pocket. She looked around and then walked to the ladies' room. She stayed there for one minute and then headed straight for the exit. She stretched her arms and pretended to yawn as she walked, trying to appear natural. This is a subconscious body movement that is frequently exhibited by people who are hiding guilt. Unfortunately for her, an off-duty police officer who had been trained in kinesics saw this. He had also seen the woman's introverted behavior and the quick detour to the bathroom. It was a curse of being in law enforcement that he could not turn off. As the shaggy suspect pushed through the front door and picked up her pace across the parking lot, a voice rang out.

"You! Right there. Stop right where you are." The voice was commanding and close behind Bertha. She could try to run for it. She could play dumb and pretend that it was an oversight. One thing she could not do was pay. She had no money. Her pockets held only the remains of smoked cigarettes that she had collected from the sidewalk. Dread, frustration, and anger filled her soul. Everyone has to eat. She turned around to see the officer with his hand extended. In it was a police badge. In the other hand, positioned by his side was a black pistol. "You need to go back inside and pay for your lunch, or you'll be eating with us tonight." A common euphemism for jail was "three hots and a cot."

Bertha dropped her head in defeat. Her stolen lunch would now cost hundreds of dollars she did not have, plus a night (or more) in jail. It was just her rotten luck. Nothing ever worked out for her. Everyone else had easy, carefree lives, but fate was determined to kick her at every opportunity. She stood still. Unable to correct the situation and unwilling to surrender made her appear obstinate.

The officer gave one more chance. "I can have a marked unit here in three minutes. It just takes one phone call. Is that really how you want this to go down?"

Bertha stood there, dirty, guilty, and in an impossible

situation. If a painless death were possible at this moment, she would have considered it.

"Sir?" Another voice rang out. It had an Asian accent. The officer looked over his shoulder. Bertha looked up. A young man wearing white kitchen clothes and an apron that could have served as a menu had opened a side door. He stood with both palms facing the officer to indicate that he meant no harm. "I can pay for her."

The officer was momentarily perplexed. In a career built around justice, this was not the norm. There was silence between the three.

The filthy criminal felt something odd in her heart. What was this? Was there a slight chance she might not go to jail? Was this hope?

"My dad owns the restaurant. He will be fine with it. I can pay for her meal," the young man added.

The officer looked puzzled and torn. "You know this woman has stolen from you...or, more accurately, your family, right? You can press charges."

"Sir, you are right to want justice. That is a good thing, but in this moment, I want to show mercy. That is also a good thing." He paused and took a tentative step closer. "Could we please let her decide?"

The officer's face twisted into disbelief. "Who? This bag lady? If you cut her a break, she's only going to think she can do it again and get away with it."

The young man considered this before speaking. "Where my family is from, we have a saying: 'He who rejects and abuses mercy will suffer the greatest punishment of all.'"

"No offense, but can a dishwasher make decisions for the owner?"

The young man smiled broadly. "Yes. He has given the restaurant to me."

36. Tight Shoes

It sounded like someone crying or maybe whimpering. I put down my newspaper and twisted my head to locate the source of the noise. Yes, there it was again. It sounded like...a man...who was exercising? But he sounded so anguished...like he was in pain. As I sat there on the park bench, my eyes began to scan for the source of the sound. There it was. A very handsome young man pedaling a shiny bicycle came up a slight incline on the path. My brain automatically made judgments and assumptions based on the information my eyes and ears received. This young man cared about appearances. Cycling was a hobby of mine, so I recognized his bike as the latest high-performance carbon fiber creation. Very nice indeed—and expensive. His shoes? They were the ones that so many celebrities had been seen wearing lately. How did he get a pair? Neither could my eyes ignore the large gold chain and pendant hanging around his neck. Wow! As he drew near, however, details emerged, and something (or rather, somethings) did not seem right. The young man noticed that I had seen him, and his face changed from anguish to apparent ease. I maintained eye contact and made a pleasant expression to indicate that I was open to meeting him and having a brief discussion. He reciprocated the unspoken social invitation and stopped the bike near my bench.

The young man smiled a bright smile and said, "Mornin'." I answered and decided to ask about his bike. It seemed like he would enjoy some admiration of his impressive wheels.

"Is that a Conpararario?"

"Yes. It is. Do you have one, too?"

I smiled and chuckled. "Oh, no. You obviously know how much those cost. Do you ride competitively?"

"No, not really. I was thinking about it, but I mostly just cruise around, getting some exercise and all."

"Hmmm. A race bike like that would be more at home in the Tour de France. Are you comfortable riding it around the park?"

The young man's demeanor changed ever so slightly. I had struck a nerve. That's when I noticed he was still sitting on the bike in an odd, tense fashion.

"Uh, well, you know, I'm still young, so I'll save comfort for when I'm older." He nodded almost imperceptibly in my direction to emphasize our age difference. There was an awkward pause in the conversation, and I could see another chink in his façade. The corners of his mouth pulled downward, and I could see a bead of sweat form near his temple.

"Are you OK?" I asked with sincere concern. "You look really uncomfortable."

He squirmed and tried to smile, but it was forced, and he swallowed hard.

"Why don't you take a break for a moment? There's plenty of room here on the bench."

The young man looked at me, then looked away as if weighing an important decision. Then, he stood up and swung his leg off of the bicycle. He stood, and a wave of relief washed over his face. He moved his legs and stretched a little. I noticed that his bicycle had no seat.

My mind tried to make sense of what I was seeing. Had this young man been riding this thing without a seat? Sitting on the tube where the seat post should have been? In moments like this, you can try to ignore the obvious under the guise of being polite, but valid concern should outweigh formality.

"Friend, why are you riding a bike with no seat? That has to be terribly uncomfortable."

He smiled nervously. "Oh, that. Well, you see, I got a really good deal on the bike. It was for sale at a police auction, you know, where they sell confiscated and unclaimed stuff. I want to buy a Conparario seat, but they are... I'm a little, well, I think they're out of stock."

Pieces were beginning to fit together in my mind. I decided to pry a little bit. "Is it worth it to ride it in this condition?"

He looked at me as if I were stupid. "This is a Conparario. They handmake these in Italy. Do you expect me to ride some cheap, big-box store bike?" An edge of offense was evident in his tone.

"You're right. It's a beautiful bike. But why don't we walk together for a few minutes? I'd like to hear more about it." My interest seemed to please him, so I stood, and we began to walk as he pushed the impressive (albeit seatless) Conparario.

We made small talk, and I asked him about what he was currently doing. He seemed to appreciate someone taking an interest in him, so he answered and expounded when the topic suited his taste. As we walked, I noticed him limping. Not limping so much as tiptoeing. It was as if his sneakers had invisible high heels that I could not see. He was hiding it well, and I didn't want to embarrass him if he had some unfortunate defect in his legs. "I notice that you're limping a little. Are you injured?"

"Injured? Oh, you mean the way I'm walking? It's my shoes. They're a little...tight."

"Well, they're very cool shoes. I saw Rex Skyler wearing those at his premiere on television last night."

"Thanks, man. I couldn't believe they were on sale. I was at the mall when I saw them on the counter at a shoe store. Some rich lady had bought them for her son, but they were the wrong size, so she was returning them. They were brand new! Apparently, returned shoes are 50% off, so I just went for it. I didn't eat much for the rest of the week, but they were absolutely worth it."

"Let me ask you. Were they your size?"

"Well, I usually wear a ten, but, you know, I can wear an eight in a pinch."

"Good pun," I said, but he didn't get the joke. This poor young man was wearing shoes two sizes too small, and he couldn't even walk normally. But, like the bike, it seemed like image and appearances took priority over sensibility.

I decided to change the subject. "That pendant is a beauty. Does it represent something?"

The young man smiled at my acknowledgment and lifted the pendant and chain from his chest. "Yeah. My family is Irish, so I had to have it when I saw our family's crest at the store."

"Wow!" I responded with feigned politeness. "And the chain is just as impressive. Did they come together?"

The young man looked around and spoke quietly. "Well, the pendant kinda wiped out my budget, so the chain is actually costume jewelry. I should be able to get a real one after my next paycheck."

I knew that a chain that size made of real gold would require several paychecks, but I appreciated his optimism. As he adjusted his shirt collar to allow for the chain, I noticed the skin around his neck was horribly irritated. It was red and swollen and looked raw in several places. "Are you OK?" I asked as I motioned toward his neck.

"What? Oh, that. Yeah, I'm not sure what's going on there. Maybe I'm allergic to my mom's laundry detergent or something."

"But it's only around your neck where the chain touches your skin."

He paused as if to consider this. "No. No, I think it's definitely the detergent."

My courtesy was wearing thin in the face of his obstinance. "Friend, I know you're very proud of your chain and your shoes and your bike. They are all very impressive. But it hurts me to see the cost you are paying to have them."

"What do you mean, 'the cost'? I told you that they're all paid for. I own them! They're mine!"

I had expected him to be defensive. I'm sure in his mind, I was criticizing the things that he held most dear. I softened my tone. "I'm not talking about money. I'm talking about the irritated skin, the sore feet, the pain in your...butt."

For a moment, I could see him considering this idea. Perhaps it was the realization that someone saw through his veneer. But would he heed kind words of counsel? No, it seemed he would not. He suddenly made a face as if I'd insulted his mother.

"You know what? You're jealous. I thought I'd come over and let you see my bike, but you're a tool. I'm outta here."

My heart broke as he threw his leg across his bike and gingerly sat on the metal protrusion. A painful grimace crossed his face as he let his weight settle onto the bike. As he pedaled away, he let out an involuntary yelp as the combination of discomforts resumed their attack.

37. TIMELESS

Life had taken a cruel turn. Ella lay there in her home, which was not as familiar and comfortable as it had once been. Squatting in her living room were unwelcome intruders: a hospital bed, an IV hanger, and a heart monitor. The steady beeping of the monitor now seemed labored and sporadic. Her life was ebbing away like water down the drain. Try as she might, there was no strength left to stop it. As she felt it depleting, a gut-wrenching melancholy engulfed her soul. She felt robbed and cheated. She was too young, and her husband was still so healthy. They should have years left, even decades. He sat at her side, holding her hand and staring into her eyes. Tears fell freely down a face that was trying to be brave. They both said "I'm sorry" for nothing they had done but for what they could not do. The looming loneliness of their impending lost decades together constricted her heart and twisted her stomach. The monitor made some faltering sounds. Her eyes closed and then flickered back open. How could she leave him? How would he manage alone?

Helplessness beyond description overwhelmed her. Her eyes closed again, and the patchy beep of the monitor began to fade in her ears. Blackness, like sleep, pulled her out of her body and away from the pain. There was silence and movement. A transformation unique to life experience was taking place. Was she feeling guilt? Or longing? She thought of her husband and the intolerable length of time before they would be together again.

Then, there was light. It was warm, pleasing to the eye, and inviting. It pulled her towards itself and radiated through her. Discomfort, uncertainty, and all things earthly were forever behind her. She knew that with a new certainty that could not be explained. Suddenly, there they were, the people she had known and said goodbye to. The absence was over. Even as the distance closed, she saw her sweet mother, a childhood friend who had drowned, and her grandfather, who had constantly fawned over her. Then she saw him, the love of her life.

If confusion were possible here, she felt it. There he was, younger but more familiar to her now than ever. She wondered how this could be. As she neared, his expression communicated that he understood. It was new to her, but he somehow silently conveyed that his being here was as it should be. New waves of peace washed over sands of serenity. *But how?* she thought as she drew near to the husband that she had just said goodbye to. As quickly as the questions formed, the answers materialized automatically in her mind.

Time on earth was like a rope that we moved along, hand over hand, in one direction only. Time here, in this new place, was like an ocean. One could swim through in any direction: forward, backward, sideways, up, down. Although he passed away twenty-seven years later than Ella, he was here now to welcome her. He assured her without words that her death had been so painful at first but that he had continued living. Acceptance and even happiness bloomed again. He also conveyed that the passing of those years was nothing now and of little consequence in comparison.

The oddest sensation was the fondness she felt for him. It was stronger but totally different. He was just as handsome as he'd been when they were dating, but there was no physical attraction. What was in its place...richer, purer, and unrestrained. There was a oneness now that they shared, just as she felt toward everyone that had been in her life.

This was the completion of a journey and the beginning of a new one. It was a rescue with no possibility of further peril. It was the release of so many needless worries and anxieties. It was the way it always should have been.

38. Trust Fall

"This is the dumbest corporate retreat I've ever been to," I said to anyone around me. We were waiting in line for what was announced as "The Ultimate Trust Fall." I'd seen this exercise before at other teambuilding events; someone stands on a low chair with their arms folded across their chest. They close their eyes and fall backward into the arms of their friends. There is the co-mingling of fear and hope in the brief moment of weightlessness. Fear that this is some cruel trick and that the others will all suddenly withdraw their safety net of hands. Or hope that they actually care about you and will do whatever it takes to keep you from falling to the ground. With well-run events (and halfway decent co-workers), the latter occurs, and everyone leaves with a shared sense of deeper trust. But this—this was a trust fall on steroids.

The organizers had built a platform that was close to forty feet tall. A staircase made of scaffolding, like at construction sites, led up to the top. The platform was wrapped in dark, black cloth to block the interior from view. One by one, the participants arrived at the top, turned around, and fell back into the abyss. Occasionally, one would have second thoughts near the top, but the line of people made retreat impossible. The stairs were too narrow, and the crowd's forward momentum was relentless. They would resist more strongly as they neared the edge, but inevitably, the force of the masses would shove them over the edge. Their descents were the opposite of graceful. Flailing arms and a horrified scream would echo as each one awkwardly succumbed to gravity.

As we made our way toward the stairs, I contemplated what I'd read in the event schedule. Under "The Ultimate Trust Fall" was a long paragraph about our CEO, or should I say fabled CEO. It spoke of how the company was started and his desire to employ as many local residents as possible. According to his bio, he was a paragon of altruism, a philanthropist extraordinaire. He'd always put the workers first, from benefits to health care to profit sharing. Surely, this guy had some skeletons in the closet. After all, who had ever seen him? His portraits are pictures drawn by children who had benefited from the frequent fundraisers hosted here. They are literally drawn with crayons. In some, he has blue hair. In another, he's wearing a huge cowboy hat. And in my personal submission for best likeness, he is wearing a pirate patch and has what appears to be a green parrot on his shoulder. Needless to say, we have no actual photos to substantiate what he looks like.

I arrive at the first flight of steps. The event schedule said that the CEO himself would be stationed at the bottom of the platform and that he personally would be available to catch each employee. Available? What was that supposed to mean? Surely, there was a Plan B just in case he was called away. Maybe a giant airbag or a team of circus acrobats? Who do you hire for such an occasion? I was nearing the top, so I would soon find out.

From here, I was able to see the faces of the employees ahead of me. The eyes of most grew wide as they saw the open maw of darkness looming ahead. The conveyor belt effect of the crowd seemed to amplify their fear with each inch moved forward. I heard another blood-curdling scream. It made the hair on my arms stand on end, and I felt like a dumbbell had been dropped inside of my stomach.

With only a minute or so before my turn came about, I began to seriously consider my faith that the CEO would be waiting...and capable of catching me. Gun to my head, I couldn't say for sure that he even exists. But I have to admit that I've always received a paycheck. It's never been late. And the company has followed through on everything listed in the policy manual. Sure, our department has had its share of fires to extinguish, and sometimes, I feel like I get dumped on. For instance, there was that time when Walter was supposed to develop a critical PowerPoint presentation for the following Monday but conveniently called in sick. Coincidentally, it was on the first day the ski resorts opened, and guess who had to develop the presentation. But that's another story. I do like Walter as a friend.

Five people ahead of me, I see a co-worker from another division. He has a reputation for being a good employee, trustworthy and friendly. I think I remember hearing that he was somehow related to the CEO but had never taken advantage of the connection. He helped at most of the fundraisers and, now that I think about it, had never really complained about his job. That was odd. If he could have pulled some strings to get a corner office, you'd think he would have. As he neared the precipice, his face was oddly serene. It was as if he was waiting in line at the coffee machine. And unlike the terrified departure of those before him, he turned his back to the pit, crossed his arms, and fell away smoothly in a disappearing, graceful arc.

I suddenly envied him. Perhaps something horrible waited

at the bottom of the pit, like long metal spikes, a giant alligator, flames, or... My imagination was running away with me. Even IF one of those things were true, he had been spared from the dread and fear that was so prevalent in most of his peers. On the other hand, no sane man would surrender so easily to such a fate. No, he had inside knowledge. He knew something the others didn't. I was confident that he truly knew the CEO and knew that he was waiting to catch him.

Two more ahead of me, each grasping wildly at handrails that were too far away. Finally, it was my turn. I'd seen that resistance was futile. This was the moment of truth. As with most moments of potential peril, my mind sped up, allowing the seconds to pass with slowness and clarity. It seemed only sensible to follow the example of my department co-worker. I surprised even myself as I turned my back to the pit, crossed my arms over my chest, and closed my eyes. Falling backward seemed effortless, and the absence of gravity was strangely welcoming. The world above receded into a tunnel of shadows as my heart began to register the excitement of anticipation. The corners of my lips lifted up into a smile.

39. Tuning In

Sleek red plastic accented with chrome, rounded edges, and an extendable antenna were Sunny's most notable features. She also had a grill-covered speaker off to one side with two knobs and a horizontal dial on the other. On the dial were numbers from 88.5 to 107.9 with little hash marks in between to delineate the myriad frequencies that were theoretically available to be tuned into. As a young (and rather lovely) radio, she was just becoming familiar with all the signals she could receive.

The whole notion of wave transmission was simultaneously simplistic and complicated. Be it radio, light, or electromagnetic energy, they all move through space very much like waves move through the ocean. They have height from trough to crest, distance between, and frequency over time. These basic attributes combine to give unique signatures to each wave action you might observe from the beach. There could be pounding surf, placid lapping, or any variation in between.

Likewise, Sunny's dial represented the full gamut of programming that was being broadcast from various places. Due to variables such as atmospheric conditions, competing frequencies, topography, and so on, it was easier to tune in to some stations than others.

At first, she was drawn to the Top 40 station. It was catchy and hip. She found herself bobbing, rocking on her little corner pads, and even turning up her volume knob when her favorites came on. But listening to forty songs took less time than you would think. It wasn't long before the first one rolled around again, and again, and again. Time to twist the tuning knob. She found the classics station, which initially seemed like an endless and inexhaustible supply of music. But something about the songs prevented them from being truly fresh. They soon took on the same appeal as leftovers in the fridge.

No problem—a slight twisting of the knob and more stops on the dial could be explored. Rap did not sit well with Sunny. Neither did metal, polka, political discussions, or weather. Classical was nice for a while. For a time, she found herself glued to the "Love Chats" channel, where callers would ask for the advice of Silvia Lovechild – relationship guru extraordinaire. But even that became tiresome. Loneliness seemed to be an endless epidemic.

One day, Sunny stumbled upon a station hidden between the hash marks of her dial. It was a man speaking words that connected with her being. They described a way through life transcending cultural trends or unpredictable weather forecasts. The words did not grow tiresome but continually introduced new concepts and an anticipation of the future. And then suddenly, the station was gone.

Storm clouds had gathered overhead and were interfering with the signal. Sunny spun her antenna about wildly, trying to regain the signal. Lightning flashed nearby, and her little speaker received the thunder as harsh static. She waggled on her little pads in hopes that changing her location would allow for better reception. But as the storm persisted, she struggled in vain to re-locate the mysterious broadcast.

When the weather cleared, she spun the dial left and right as she strained to hear the familiar voice. For some reason, the stations she once enjoyed were now grating to her circuits. She wondered how she had once enjoyed such frivolity. *Where are you?* She thought in frustration as she frantically scoured the dial. Her little indicator flew over the numbers and stopped sporadically. This was not working.

Sunny took a deep breath and sat very still. Once calm, she turned the knob with a painful slowness. She craned her antenna as the warbly signals grew and faded. Several trips along the dial revealed only silence, static, and irritation. Had she imagined the whole thing?

She decided to go back to the exact spot where she had been. Unlike her cousin, the Walkman, mobility was not her strong suit. She waddled clumsily back to the place on the shelf where she had been when she last heard the words. Again, she stretched out her antenna and slowly turned the dial once more.

There it was! Sunny immediately recognized the voice. It was not a clear signal, but relief flooded her batteries. She dared not move as she made a mental note of the frequency. She absorbed the words and basked in the feeling of completion, slowly replacing her restlessness. Suddenly, the signal wavered, and she leaned at precarious angles, trying to find just the right position. There, that was better.

Other radios passed by and thought it was odd that she was in such a peculiar posture. Most moved past, whereas others turned up their volume knobs to be annoying. Sunny remained poised and guarded. She tried to tell other radios about this mesmerizing program, but none seemed interested. She admitted that if she had not stumbled across this jewel, she too would be endlessly searching for distraction.

By accident, Sunny discovered that movement could improve or worsen her signal strength. And so it began that she was continually shifting and hopping toward the signal so that she might secure a connection. Sometimes storms caused temporary separation silence, but she became more adept at finding the station. As she gained higher ground, it became even easier.

Over time, her red veneer began to fade into a Pepto Bismol pink. Her antenna had a notable bend and kink about halfway up. The hash marks on her dials were worn smooth, and her batteries were registering far less than their indicated 1.5 volts. Sunny's fascination with the words had superseded those concerns. She now stood at the summit of a hill directly underneath the transmission tower. A little zig-zag trail in the dirt and grass led down the hill and into the sea of noises she had worked so hard to escape.

40. WORMS APLENTY

The shells served a very specific purpose for their occupants. Two of them in this case. One grew very content inside, whereas the other grew restless. For the latter, it all just became a bit stuffy.

"Can you breathe over there? It's getting a bit tight at my place."

The question roused Rob from his slumber. "Breathe? I suppose so. I hadn't really given it any thought."

"How are you not getting claustrophobic?" Jay groaned. "I feel like my legs are beginning to cramp."

Rob considered this. Perhaps it was a bit tight, but it felt like security to him. It was dark, peaceful, and quiet except for Jay's frequent grumblings. Everything he needed was within arm's reach—or rather, wing's reach. His stomach felt swimmy as he suddenly felt his den shift. It was probably Jay moving about again. Didn't Jay realize that could cause problems?

"I don't think I can stand much more of this," groaned Jay. It wasn't so much a complaint as it was a statement. "Ummmpph!"

Rob felt a jolt. "What are you doing, Jay? Be still!"

" Ummmpph!"

"Jay?"

"*Ummmpph!*"

There was an unusual cracking noise. Rob's heart froze for a moment. That sound should never be heard. "Jay?"

"Errrr, Ummmph, Arrrrgghh, *Yes!*" And with that last effort, Jay's feathered head popped out dead center at the top like a periscope. His round, black eyes blinked as he swiveled around, taking in the scenery.

"Rob! You gotta see this! This is amazing! This is the first time I've seen something like this! There are...um, I don't know what they are. But I'm gonna find out!"

"Jay! What have you done? You can't be outside! It's... it's... you just don't do that!"

"Rob, it's time. Did you not feel this coming? Let me get the rest of me out, and then I'll help you."

Rob felt more jostling. His heart pounded with fear. He pushed his little wings against both sides to steady himself. He felt panic. "Jay, stop it right now! You could break my shell!"

Jay wiggled out and looked back at the broken white shards with mixed feelings. It had been nice, he supposed. But if change leads to improvement, so be it.

He waddled a bit on the uneven tapestry of twigs but soon found that by using his tiny talons, he could move about quite freely. He moved to the bowl-like perimeter and gazed over the edge. *Wow! We are so high up!*

"Rob! I'm serious. You've gotta see this!" He returned to his brother's shell and gave it a hard whack with the pointy implement positioned just beyond his eyes.

"Stop it!" Jay shouted. "You can wreck your home, but leave mine alone!"

The tone of Rob's words caused him to stop. Yes, the outside world was amazing, but perhaps it should be discovered at one's own pace.

"Sorry, bro. I just got excited."

Rob could hear his brother moving about. He could also hear the exclamations, the oohs and aahs. A new sentiment stirred within his little mind. A small part of him...wanted what Jay had. He wanted to see what Jay saw and experience what Jay felt. But no. He was born inside of the shell, and the shell was where he would stay.

Minutes later, there was a whooshing sound. It was familiar to Rob, and it usually preceded a welcome warmth.

"Mom!" It was Jay again. "Mom! Look! I'm out of the shell!"

"Very good, Jay. Just look at you! You are quite the handsome sparrow, just like your father. I expected this to be the day, so I brought breakfast."

"Whoa! What are these? Why are they moving?"

"They're called worms. And these are as fresh as they get. Try one."

Rob could hear the conversation, the smacking, and then the moans of fulfillment. Another pang of jealousy.

"How about your brother? Have you heard from him today?"

"He, um, I think he needs a little more baking."

"Hmmm." His mother twisted her beak with concern and then sat down gently on the egg with great grace.

Now, Rob felt something else. He would have recognized the feelings as embarrassment and shame if he had been more developed. *Jay doesn't need any more baking,* he thought sarcastically.

Rob eventually made it out of his shell. It was a long, traumatic process, but once outside, he headed straight for the protection of his mother's wings. She enjoyed coddling him. She also enjoyed watching Jay strut around and experiment with his wings.

"So, I've seen you use these. What's the deal?" piped Jay.

"You are going to love them, Jay," answered his mother.

"They are what set us apart from all of the other animals. The gift of flight. They say that all creatures envy us and dream of doing what we do, but you mustn't let it go to your head."

Jay looked again at his wings and pondered this. They just seemed normal to him.

Twelve days later, Jay stood on the edge of the nest. Even looking at his brother on the brink of certain death gave Rob vertigo. Jay's mother continued giving instructions. "OK. One quick step, and then spread your wings out as far as you can. Keep your head down, and you'll feel lift starting to take place as you gain speed. Look where you want to go; your body will automatically control your glide path. It's really quite exci—." And before she could finish, he was gone.

The sound of wind whistled past Jay's ears. He felt the wind in his feathers and opened his eyes wide to fully take in the moment. Faster and faster, lower and lower. *What a rush!* As the ground neared, Jay remembered his mom's guidance. He looked upward at a nearby branch, and his tailfeathers tilted up, changing his angle of descent. As he leveled out, he began to swim through the air with quick, powerful strokes. He found that less effort on the right wing caused him to turn that way, and the same for the left. He was gone for a full fifteen minutes before touching down on the rim of his nest.

Rob was surprised by how his brother suddenly looked very mature and able. *Stupid Jay.* Rob saw no reason to fly. Thanks to his mom, he had enough worms (for now). He tried to ignore how hard she worked to feed him as well as herself. But life was comfortable, predictable, and safe.

As time passed, Rob needed more worms to support his unfortunate habit of growing. Jay had virtually moved out. He would pop in from time to time, share stories of his latest adventures and close calls, and then he'd be off again. His mom spent more and more time out searching. She looked thinner. He looked up as he heard the whoosh of wings approaching.

Just great. Here's Mr. Wonderful.

Jay looked amazing. His brown-over-gray feathers stood out against the sky but complemented the fauna equally well. It's tough when you envy someone you resent.

"Hey, Jay. Whatcha' been up to?"

Jay's wings swirled around the small nest as he began his newest tale. He was so animated. "Rob, you don't know what you're missing. The world is *amazing*! This morning, there was a lady down at the park. She was totally throwing perfectly good French fries on the ground. It was a feast! And that rain shower last night? Apparently, worms come to the surface when the ground gets wet. Can you say smorgasbord, or what? And don't get me started about the bugs!"

Rob didn't realize how long his small, beaked face had become. Jay noticed and suddenly became serious. "Sorry, bro. I know that you're struggling a little bit."

Rob felt flushed with anger. "Struggling? You think I'm struggling?" His voice had grown shrill.

Jay looked around sheepishly. "Keep it down, dude! The neighbors are looking." Jay stooped low near his brother and spoke just above a whisper. "Rob, I am not trying to hurt your feelings. It's just that we were made to fly. It's who we are. It's what we do. You know mom and I love you like crazy, but we need to get you out there!" His tone escalated with excitement. He was motioning out toward the wild blue yonder, longing to return there but knowing he should be here doing what he could. Jay refocused and looked his brother in the eye. He grinned playfully and said, "OK. Tell me what's going on in that little bird brain of yours."

Rob felt something inside that he knew didn't belong. He would have had it surgically removed if he could have identified it. But no medical doctor could help with this issue. He needed a counselor. He needed a friend. He looked down before uttering, "I'm afraid."

Jay's head ticked backward with surprise. "Afraid? Afraid of what?" He was mindful of his tone so as not to sound disapproving.

"Of everything, I guess." Jay's silence and attention goaded Rob to expound. "I'm afraid of crashing. I'm afraid of cats. I'm afraid of tornados. I'm afraid of not being able to build a nest. I'm afraid of starving to death."

Jay held his wings up like two stop signs. "Whoa, whoa, whoa. Let's slow down a little bit. I appreciate you sharing this, but I don't understand. Why are you afraid of these things?"

Rob considered this. He thought it should have been obvious to everyone, but maybe not. "I'm afraid of the uncertainty. I'm afraid of pain."

Jay felt sincere compassion for his younger brother. He'd recognized his own knack for picking up new things easily. His brother, on the other hand, was less Alpha and more Omega. Jay knew then and there what he had to do. "Let's try a breathing exercise. I saw some humans doing this on a rooftop the other day."

It didn't sound too dangerous, so Rob stood up.

"Alright. Now close your eyes and let your wings hang loosely by your sides."

Rob complied and tried to relax.

"Alright. Now step forward with your right leg, getting a good lunge stretch."

Rob obeyed and thought about how pleasant Jay could be when he tried.

"Now, bring your left leg forward with both feet together. Center yourself. Now, step forward with your left leg. Deeeep stretch."

This is working. I do feel calmer. With eyes closed, Rob didn't realize he was moving closer to the edge of the nest. Jay was gradually moving around behind him.

"Now, bring your right leg forward. Both feet together. Forward fold..."

"Ahhhhhhh!" There had been a sharp push from behind, and now he was tumbling beak over tail. His eyes snapped open. A blur of leaves, trees, and sky flashed past. He thrashed about wildly with his talons but grabbed only air. A strange blend of impotence, dread, and acceptance filled his soul. And then there was someone else.

Jay was in a nosedive, expertly matching his speed and moving under Rob's chest. With a quick flip of his tail, both their bodies were stabilizing and leveling out.

"Wings out!" ordered Jay with a shocking amount of force.

Rob obeyed in an instant. Their bodies separated. Jay was flying level, which meant that he was going up!

"Now flap! Hard!" Jay shouted in encouragement.

Rob rolled his wings forward and upward, downward and backward. Forward and upward, downward and backward. He was a little wobbly but, overall, not too shabby. He experimented with the left and right controls and suddenly felt like he'd been doing this his whole life. "This is wonderful!" he shouted to himself, to Jay, and to anyone listening. To the bipeds below, it was a cheerful series of chirps and whistles.

Jay drew alongside him, and they engaged in a game of Follow the Leader. They went under ladders, buzzed a neighborhood cat, and skimmed just over the surface of a pond; nowhere was off limits.

After several minutes, they landed on a statue whose white glaze indicated that this was a popular spot for their kind. Rob was breathing hard but smiling. He looked at Jay with a puzzled expression. *Shouldn't I be mad at this guy? Did he not trick me and almost kill me?* But for some reason, he was not. Resentment seemed to dissipate like clouds after a storm had passed.

"Mom's going to be super proud of you," Jay cheeped.

Rob imagined this pleasant image in his mind.

"And I am, too."

"But, I...,"

"It doesn't matter how you got here. You're here. Thank you for letting me be a part of it."

Rob nudged him playfully with his wing. "I don't think I had much of a choice."

They enjoyed the silence for a few minutes before Rob spoke up.

"So, about the food and shelter? Am I silly to be worried about those too?"

Acknowledgments

Several people deserve to be recognized for their assistance, encouragement, and contributions to this book. My publisher, Publish Authority, has the incredible ability to turn a dream into reality. Frank Eastland and Raeghan Rebstock have held my hand and guided me through this first publishing experience. The knowledge they have imparted will serve me for years to come. Janet Silburn, my editor, has transformed, refined, and improved my manuscript almost to the point of being my co-author. My friend Scott Cottrell encouraged me, shared lessons from his publishing experience, and made the crucial introduction to Publish Authority.

Endless thanks go to the people who have enriched my life with their friendship. Lastly, I would likely not know any success without the faithful support of my sweet wife, Shanna. She will always be my favorite of all God's blessings.

AUTHOR'S QR CODE

SCAN ME

About the Author

John Cleveland has had several things shape his life. Growing up in Alabama, serving in the Army Reserves, completing a career with the Highway Patrol, and moving to the western edge of the Rocky Mountains upon retirement have been the banal events. Being married to his sweet Shanna, traveling often to enjoy this world, making memories with friends, and knowing God are the things he wants to remember when he is old.

For more about the author, you are invited to visit his website at JCWriting.com.

Glossary

In case you're unfamiliar with some of the nautical terms used in these stories, below are a few terms defined by the author.

Bailing Bucket: A container to scoop water from the bottom of a boat and toss it overboard.

Boom: The horizontal pole that attaches to the mast. It holds the bottom of the sail in place and can be swiveled to catch the wind.

Bridge: The room where the captain controls everything aboard their ship. It typically contains the helm (or steering wheel), throttle, radio, radar, etc.

Bulkhead: The walls within the interior of a ship. They are often watertight to help the boat stay afloat in case some other area springs a leak.

Crow's nest: A small bucket mounted near the top of a mast. A sailor would stand or sit inside and be on the lookout for objects on the water, land, or enemy ships.

Deck: The highest outside surface of a ship where you typically walk or work.

Forecastle: The main structure of a motorized ship. It contains the bridge and helm where the captain operates the boat.

Gunwale: (pronounced "gunnel" like "funnel") The top edges or sides of a boat.

Helm: The steering wheel of the boat. Fancier versions are made of ornate wood with protruding knobs to improve grip.

Hull: The main outer portion of the boat. The hull can be made of steel, wood, fiberglass, tree bark, or even cloth! You don't want any holes in your hull.

In Irons: A sailing term that describes the position of the sail when it is catching no wind. It typically flaps uselessly downwind and is used when preparing to launch or dock.

Mast: The tall pole protruding from a sailboat that holds the sail.

Port: The left-hand side of a boat when facing the bow (front). It's easy to remember because both "port" and "left" contain four letters.

Rigging: The ropes and pulleys to raise, lower, and adjust the sails.

Starboard: The right-hand side of a boat. It's easy to remember because "right" and "starboard" are longer words than "left" and "port."

Throttle: The lever which controls the speed of the engine(s).

Throttle Stop: As far forward as the throttle lever will go.

Yardarm: The outer edges of the tallest boom attached to the mast of a sailing ship. It would be one of the last parts of a sinking ship to go underwater.

Also by John Cleveland

7: A sampler from the larger collection, 40

Modern Parables about Faith, God, and Human Nature

Discover inspiration in the palm of your hand with this pocket-size treasure. The seven stories in this collection, handpicked from the extensive anthology "40," are a beacon of hope and wisdom. Designed as a delightful giveaway, share this book of tales with friends, family, or anyone in need of a spark.

THANK YOU FOR READING

If you enjoyed 40, we invite you to leave a review online and share your thoughts and reactions with friends and family.

Publish Authority

Printed in the USA
CPSIA information can be obtained
at www.ICGtesting.com
LVHW051124070624
782592LV00012B/364